Do Preserve

Make your own jams, chutneys, pickles and cordials

Happy preserving!

Mimi

Anja Dunk
Jen Goss
Mimi Beaven

Published by
The Do Book Company 2016
Works in Progress Publishing Ltd
thedobook.co

Text copyright © Anja Dunk,
Jen Goss, Mimi Beaven 2016
Photography copyright
© Richard Beaven 2016

A CIP catalogue record for this book
is available from the British Library

ISBN 978-1-907974-24-3

1 3 5 7 9 10 8 6 4 2

To find out more about our company,
books and authors, please visit
thedobook.co or follow us **@dobookco**

5% of our proceeds from the
sale of this book is given to
The Do Lectures to help it achieve
its aim of making positive change
thedolectures.com

Cover designed by James Victore
Book designed and set by Ratiotype

Printed and bound by Livonia Print Ltd
on Munken, an FSC-certified paper

For our friend Clare

Books in the series:

Do Beekeeping
The secret to happy honeybees
Orren Fox

Do Birth
A gentle guide to labour and childbirth
Caroline Flint

Do Breathe
Calm your mind. Find focus.
Get stuff done
Michael Townsend Williams

Do Design
Why beauty is key to everything
Alan Moore

Do Disrupt
Change the status quo. Or become it
Mark Shayler

Do Fly
Find your way. Make a living.
Be your best self
Gavin Strange

Do Grow
Start with 10 simple vegetables
Alice Holden

Do Improvise
Less push. More pause. Better results.
A new approach to work (and life)
Robert Poynton

Do Lead
Share your vision. Inspire others.
Achieve the impossible
Les McKeown

Do Preserve
Make your own jams, chutneys, pickles
and cordials
Anja Dunk, Jen Goss, Mimi Beaven

Do Protect
Legal advice for startups
Johnathan Rees

Do Purpose
Why brands with a purpose do better
and matter more
David Hieatt

Do Sourdough
Slow bread for busy lives
Andrew Whitley

Do Story
How to tell your story so the world listens
Bobette Buster

Available in print and digital formats
from bookshops, online retailers
or via our website:
thedobook.co

To hear about events and forthcoming
titles, you can find us on Facebook,
on Twitter and Instagram @dobookco,
or subscribe to our newsletter

Contents

Apple strudel filling (recipe page 26)

Introduction

Sowing seeds, planting out, harvesting fruit and vegetables, perusing the hedgerows and roadside stalls or local produce markets; many of us have followed some or all of these traditions and rituals for decades. Happily many more of us are following the seasons once again – understanding the value and environmental benefit of seasonality.

To make the most of bounteous harvests when they are upon us we need to store some away. There is so much delight in making a pot of jam or chutney, to eat later or give away as a gift.

There are many ways to preserve – people all over the globe have been doing so for centuries. In this book we will cover the basics. Our aim is to try and make preserving accessible to all, whether you live in a small urban apartment or a house with a garden. The recipes in this book have been written with everyone in mind – please don't be put off by images of hundreds of empty jars waiting to be filled. Unless you have a large garden or allotment you are not going to be wondering what to do with 10kg of tomatoes. It is more likely you'll have a small bag of foraged blackberries or some apples from a friend's garden and are looking for a few ideas.

When we preserve we slow down the natural process of decay. There are four elements we battle with to be able to store our food for longer: bacteria, mould, yeasts and enzymes. In *Do Preserve* we use sugar, vinegar, alcohol, salt and oil as basic preserving agents, and bottling and drying as processes to store produce. You'll find that each has its own chapter and accompanying recipes. There's also a separate chapter on sugar-free preserving. These are by no means the only methods – others include curing and smoking – but due to space restrictions we'll have to leave that for another book!

This book has been written by three of us – Anja, Jen and Mimi – cooks who became friends through our shared passion for preserving nature's bounty and swapping recipes. We originally met through the Do Lectures, where we have all cooked at different times (Anja and Jen at the Do Lectures in Wales and Mimi at Do USA).

Even though we each assumed responsibility for writing a particular section of the book, we all contributed recipes, so it's very much a joint effort. If you're interested in who contributed which recipe, they are marked with our initials in the list of recipes at the start of each chapter.

So before we begin, let's look at what you need to get started.

Preserving

The basic equipment you will need is:

— **The biggest pan you can get hold of** – but bear in mind you can make a couple of jars in a normal-sized pan. Go for a non-corrosive pan such as stainless steel or copper, especially when using vinegar and salt as these preserving agents can corrode aluminium pans

— **Funnel** – two are useful: one wide-mouthed, one regular

— **Jars and bottles** – recycled ones are great, an average jar holds 250ml (half a US pint), so these would be good to get started

— **Labels** – don't forget them! Always label straight away to ensure you can enjoy your hard work for as long as possible. An unlabelled jar will lose some of its attractiveness if you don't know what it is or when you made it.

— **Ladle**

— **Measuring jug**

— **Mixing bowl** – again, go for a non-corrosive bowl such as glass, ceramic or stainless steel when using vinegar and salt

— **Muslin** – a pack of baby muslin squares are a practical option, alternatively you can buy in kitchen shops

— **Scales**

— **Sieve**

— **Thermometer** (useful but not essential)

— **Wooden spoon**

A note about muslin bags

When making jellies (as we will in chapter 1), you will need to use a muslin/jelly bag or piece of muslin to strain the juices of the fruit into a bowl or jug – see photograph on page 32. To set up, bring the four corners of the muslin together holding the fruit in, and tie to the handle of a wall cupboard if you have one. Alternatively place a chair upside down on a table, tie the four corners of the muslin to the four legs and collect the juices underneath in a bowl or jug. You can also buy a jam or jelly strainer to place the muslin on.

Sterilising

You do not need a large kitchen, massive pots and pans, and expensive equipment to make a couple of jars of chutney. But you do need a clean kitchen, freshly sterilised jars and lids, and clean sterile equipment. This will give you a head start against the bacteria that are everywhere in our everyday lives.

To sterilise jars and equipment simply boil them in a pan of water for 10 minutes. Jars can also be put in the oven at 140°C / 280°F / Gas mark 1 for 20 minutes. Recycled jars and bottles are great to use, but do check that the lids are not damaged. And always use new lids when bottling/canning. You'll find further details in chapter 3.

Now you know what you will need, let's begin by having a look at the simplest form of preserving and how it all works.

1
Sugar

Recipes

Sugar

It is always good to consider what a healthy diet consists of, what is good for the environment and what is great to eat. We cannot ignore the current understanding of what a healthy diet is made up of and the importance of cutting down on sugar overall, especially the 'hidden' sugars in processed foods – it's the right way to go. Many things are bad for your health, but food cooked from scratch, full of healthy fruit and vegetables, without additives and chemical preservatives, is good for you, as long as you don't eat too much. A balanced diet is what is important for all.

We know that people from the earliest cultures preserved with sugar and that they would not only store fruit in honey for their larder, but also trade with it. In cultures where there wasn't enough sun to dry the fruits, the fruit and sugar would be heated up together to make jams. Sugar draws water from microbes present in fruit, which then dehydrate and die.

There needs to be at least 60 per cent sugar present to create this environment, but recipes will vary depending on the fruit or vegetable. If you don't add enough sugar to a preserve it will take longer to boil and you will lose the colour, flavour and texture of the fruit. Some of the sugar percentage will occur naturally in the fruit sugar known as fructose, hence the different ratios in different recipes.

Principally we use sugar to make one of our favourite breakfast spreads, the humble jam, but we can use sugar to help preserve all sorts of other fun and delicious things, such as:

— **Butter** – a smooth and creamy spread created by slow-cooking fruit and sugar, then passing the mixture through a sieve or squeezing through a muslin

— **Cheese** – made with fruit and sugar and cooked slowly until sticky and firm

— **Compote** – whole fruit cooked in syrup, sometimes with spices; this can also be made without sugar

— **Conserve** – a mixture of sugar and whole fruit, it has a thick chunky texture

— **Coulis** – made by mixing fruit and sugar and then puréeing

— **Jelly** – a clear mixture of fruit juice and sugar; you can also add tea, wine, fruit, flowers or herbs

— **Marmalade** – a citrus spread made from the peel and pulp of the fruit boiled with sugar and water

— **Preserves** – spreads that have chunks of fruit surrounded by jelly

— **Spread** – a smooth product, created by slow cooking, with no added sugar

Warming the sugar

Sometimes we want to keep the freshness and integrity of the fruit as intact as possible – particularly when making jams with fragile fruits that take little time to cook. One technique is to warm the sugar before adding to the pan. Some people do this and others don't. For the recipes that follow, it is optional. To warm the sugar, preheat the oven to 180°C/350°F/Gas mark 4, then place the sugar evenly on a baking sheet and heat in the oven for 4 minutes.

Setting point – for all jams and jellies

There is one important thing you need to know when preserving with sugar and that is the setting point.

This is simple as long as you have the correct ratio of sugar to fruit, your jam should set once it is cooked. There are two different ways you can check if your jam is ready:

Wrinkle test
When you start cooking, place a small plate in the fridge or freezer to cool. A good indicator of when your jam is nearly ready is that the bubbles change slightly and it flows differently when you stir it. When you think your jam is ready, drop a small amount onto the plate and allow it to cool. Once cool, push your finger through the jam. If it wrinkles, you have reached the setting point. While you are testing the jam, make sure the heat is turned off so it doesn't continue cooking.

Thermometer
Alternatively, once the jam is boiling, place a sugar or jam thermometer into the pan. It will need to reach 104.5°C (220°F) for the setting point.

Wrinkle test
When you think your jam is ready, drop a small amount onto the
cold plate and allow it to cool. Once cool, push your finger through
the jam. If it wrinkles, you have reached the setting point

Types of sugars

There are different kinds of specialised sugars, but please don't be put off or intimidated; you can use normal granulated sugar in all recipes and it will still work.

Jam sugar

Jam sugar has pectin and sometimes also citric acid added. Pectin exists naturally in some fruits – plums, damsons, gooseberries, apples, pears, quince and citrus. Pectin acts as a gelling agent in jams and jellies. This sugar is good for strawberry and rhubarb jams. Many jam makers avoid the artificial pectin and add the juice of a lemon or a chopped-up apple (pips in – they are high in pectin) to introduce natural gelling agents.

Granulated sugar

A good all-round cheap sugar to use in most preserving, it is refined and bleached. You can buy a more expensive unrefined one if you wish (such as Billington's in the UK). Unrefined sugars have a more natural colour.

Brown sugar

Light and dark brown sugars are refined sugar bathed in molasses, while demerara sugar is a large-grained raw sugar. These brown sugars will change the colour and taste in any preserve and can overwhelm some fruits. Light or dark brown sugar is delicious in chutneys and demerara is perfect for marmalade.

Nothing quite beats learning by doing, so – assuming you now have your basic equipment, some fruit and a bit of time – we're going straight into some of our favourite recipes that preserve gorgeous seasonal fruits by using sugar.

Bramble Yum
Sept '14

Bramble jelly

We have a tradition in our family: we give jars of this away for Christmas presents and, for ourselves, we open the first one on Christmas Day to have with croissants and bubbly in the morning... at least, we try and wait that long. This is a real waft of summer on a cold, grey morning, on your porridge, toast or with some thick Greek yogurt and nuts as a dessert. It's a lovely pastime to gather the fruit on a walk with friends and family.

Makes 500ml (1 US pint)
—

1kg (2¼lb) blackberries
Granulated sugar – for quantities see below
1 lemon

1. Put the blackberries with 2 tablespoons of water into a large pan and cook until completely soft. Remove from the heat and pour the fruit through a muslin tied up and suspended over a large jug or bowl to collect the juice. Do not squeeze the fruit as this will make the jelly cloudy. Leave for at least 4 hours – or overnight if possible.

2. Measure the juice. For every 500ml (1 US pint) of juice add 400g (14oz) sugar; add the juice of the lemon and warm up slowly to dissolve the sugar. Bring to the boil and keep boiling until setting point is reached. Pour into sterilised jars and seal.

Keeps for one year. Once opened, refrigerate and eat within three months.

Mulberry jam with strawberries

Mulberries hold their shape when cooked, so the strawberries here serve to provide body for the jam, rather than a strong flavour. The mulberries make a deep purple jam and their seeds add a wonderful popping texture.

Makes approx. 1 litre (2 US pints)

—

800g (1¾lb) sugar
400g (14oz) strawberries
600g (1lb 5oz) mulberries
150ml (⅔ cup) lemon juice
      (roughly juice of 2½ large lemons)

1. Put the sugar and strawberries into a saucepan and crush with a potato masher for 2 minutes until the juices are released. Add the mulberries and bring to the boil over a medium heat, stirring occasionally with a wooden spoon to prevent the jam from sticking to the bottom of the pan. Once boiling, add the lemon juice. Boil rapidly for about 20 minutes, stirring from time to time. Test for setting point.

2. Remove the pan from the heat. Don't worry about any scum that might have formed on the surface, stir the jam with a wooden spoon to disperse it. Pour the jam into warm sterilised jars and seal immediately.

Store in a cool, dark place for up to a year. Once opened, refrigerate and eat within three months.

Rhubarb, cardamom and orange jam

The flavours for this jam are inspired by Meera Sodha's recipe for spiced baked rhubarb. The sharp rhubarb carries the perfumed flavour of cardamom so well. I enjoy this spooned over strained yogurt or ice cream just as much as with hot buttered toast.

Makes approx. 750ml (1½ us pints)
—

**1kg (2¼lb) rhubarb, trimmed and chopped
into 1cm (½ inch) chunks
1kg (2¼lb) sugar
Zest of 1 orange
Juice of 2 small oranges (150ml, ⅔ cup)
Seeds from 8 cardamom pods**

1. Place all the ingredients into a large saucepan and bring to the boil, stirring every so often to ensure the sugar dissolves and the jam does not catch on the bottom of the pan. Boil for 20–25 minutes, stirring occasionally, until setting point is reached. Skim off any scum if needed.

2. Remove from the heat, pour into warm sterilised jars and seal.

Store in a cool, dark place. Keeps well for up to one year. Once opened, store in the fridge and use within three months.

Strudel filling

Desserts filled with apples come in various guises. One little jar of this on your shelf makes a simple apple strudel just five minutes away from going in the oven. This filling can also be used in crumbles, pies and cobblers.

Makes approx. 1.2 litres (2½ US pints)
—

1.75kg (4lb) eating apples (any variety – but I use ruby-red McIntosh or Cox's Orange Pippin)
50g (2oz) raisins
300g (11oz) brown sugar
1 tsp mixed spice
30ml (2 tbsp) dark rum (optional)
5ml (1 tsp) vanilla extract

SUGAR

1. Heat the oven to 200°C / 400°F / Gas mark 6.

2. Peel, core and roughly chop the apples. Place them on a baking tray, scatter over the raisins, sprinkle with brown sugar and spices, then pour over the rum and vanilla extract. Toss everything with your hands so the apples are well coated with sugar and spice.

3. Cover the tray loosely with foil and place in the centre of the oven to bake for 40–45 minutes, turning halfway through, until the apples have softened but still hold their shape.

4. The apples will have drawn quite a bit of liquid, this is normal. Pack the hot apples into sterilised jars, topping up with the liquid – it should just cover the apples. Tap the jar on the work surface to bring any air bubbles to the surface. Seal immediately.

Store in a cool, dark place. Keeps well for up to six months.
Once opened, store in the fridge and use within three days.

How to make a simple strudel

1. Lay out a piece of pre-rolled puff pastry onto a prepared baking tray. Spread the contents of a jar over half the pastry, leaving a 1cm (½ inch) border around the edges.

2. Brush the border with egg wash and fold the pastry over the top of the apple filling; press down along the sides to seal the filling in. Slash the top with a knife at 3cm (1¼ inch) intervals (this helps release the steam as well as provide a pretty pattern).

3. Bake in the centre of a preheated oven (200°C / 400°F / Gas mark 6) for 20–25 minutes until the top is golden. Enjoy with whipped cream or ice cream.

SUGAR

Damson jam in the oven

This is my favourite jam – chewy and caramelly. It is so versatile, I use it in lots of desserts and even in sauces.

The quantities here sound like a lot, but once the fruit is stoned it makes a manageable amount. Damsons are known as clingstone fruit, which, as the name suggests, means they can be quite hard to stone. But the end result of this jam will really be worth the extra effort. It may seem a little odd to remove the stones and then add 20 of them back to the mix, but there is a good reason for this. The stones impart a lovely mellow almondy flavour to the jam – it's easy to remove them after cooking, especially if you know exactly how many you put in.

Makes approx. 1.2 litres (2½ us pints)

—

**3kg (6lb 10oz) damsons, fully ripe,
    hold back 20 damson stones**
450g (1lb) sugar
30ml (2 tbsp) white wine vinegar

1. Heat the oven to 200°c /400°f / Gas mark 6.

2. Stone the damsons by making a slit down the crease and scooping the stone out with a knife, or if the damsons are really soft you can just squeeze the stone out with your fingers. You will need two large baking trays to lay this quantity of fruit and the stones on. Scatter the sugar evenly over the top, followed by a sprinkling of white wine vinegar.

3. Place in the centre of the oven for 45 minutes. Take the damsons out of the oven, remove the stones, stir and spoon into hot sterilised jars. Seal immediately.

Store in a cool, dark place for up to one year. Once opened, refrigerate and eat within three months.

Blackberry and Bramley apple butter

A butter is essentially a spread in which the proportion of fruit is higher than the sugar. Think of it as a cross between a jelly and a compote. The beauty of a butter is that you get instant results, unlike a jelly, which needs to drip overnight. You can use any cooking apple and berry combination – elderberries, late-autumn raspberries and loganberries work equally well.

Makes approx. 1.2 litres (2½ us pints)

—

500g (1lb 2oz) blackberries
1kg (2¼lb) cooking apples, roughly chopped
1.2 litres (4¾ cups) water
750g (1lb 10oz) sugar
60ml (4 tbsp) lemon juice (roughly the juice of 1 lemon)

1. Put the blackberries, apples (no need to de-core and peel) and water into a large pan and cook over a medium-high heat for about 20 minutes until the apples have broken down into a mush.

2. Pass the fruit pulp through a sieve over a large bowl – discard the excess pulp once no more juice comes out. You should be left with about 1700ml (approx. 3½ us pints) of smooth, liquid fruit pulp.

3. Tip the fruit pulp back into the pan along with the sugar and lemon juice. Boil for about 30 minutes over a medium-high heat. Stir occasionally to ensure the fruit doesn't stick to the bottom of the pan. When you notice the blip of bubbles coming to the surface slowing down and the size of the bubbles increasing, the butter is ready.

4. Pour the butter into hot sterilised jars. Seal immediately.

Store in a cool, dark place for up to one year. Once opened, refrigerate and eat within three months.

SUGAR

Black fig jam with vanilla and lime

Come mid-September in Britain, fig trees are laden with ripe fruit. Our neighbour has a tree, the branches of which hang over into our garden. It is with these 'liberated' figs belonging to next door that I first made this jam. This is a soft-set jam as the pectin and acid levels of figs is quite low.

Makes approx. 1 litre (2 US pints)
—

1kg (2¼lb) black figs, cut into quarters
Zest and juice of 2 limes (100ml, about ½ cup)
600g (1lb 5oz) sugar
1 vanilla pod, split lengthways

SUGAR

1. Place the figs, lime zest, sugar and vanilla pod into a large pan. As there is no added liquid at this stage you will need to stir everything together quite vigorously, crushing the figs with a wooden spoon to moisten the mix.

2. Set on a high heat and bring to the boil (this should only take five minutes), stirring all the time to dissolve the sugar, draw out as much moisture from the fruit as possible and to avoid burning.

3. Once boiling, turn the heat down to medium-high and let the contents of the pan bubble away for 25 minutes until it has become thick and gloopy (I don't bother to do the wrinkle test with this jam).

4. Take the pan off the heat and stir in the lime juice. Pour into hot sterilised jars and seal immediately.

Store in a cool, dark place for up to a year. Once opened, store in the fridge and eat within three months.

Redcurrant jelly with lemon and vanilla

The inspiration for this jelly comes from a favourite German coffee cake of mine – a redcurrant streusel cake, which is flavoured with lemon zest and vanilla sugar. I normally make the cake with the first redcurrant harvest and miss eating it until the next year comes around. Through making this jam, I get to experience its wonderful flavours all year round. Perfect on crumpets, toast, scones, pancakes and porridge, and especially good in jam tarts. This recipe is based on the old tried and tested method of using 450g of sugar per 600ml of measured juice.

Makes approx. 1 litre (2 US pints)
—

1kg (2¼lb) redcurrants
1 vanilla pod, split lengthways
6 strips of lemon zest (tip: I use a potato peeler)
400ml (1¾ cups) water
Sugar as required

1. Place the redcurrants, vanilla pod and lemon zest in a large saucepan and cover with the water. Bring to the boil, turn the heat down and simmer until tender – this will take about 40 minutes. Strain overnight through a jelly bag or muslin (see page 12). Do not squeeze the liquid through the cloth, however tempting it is (this is a slow process, one drip at a time), as it will result in a cloudy jelly.

2. Measure the juice – you will need 450g (approx. 1lb) of sugar per 600ml (approx. 1¼ US pints) of liquid. Pour the redcurrant juice into a large pan and bring to the boil. Tip in the sugar and stir to dissolve. Boil rapidly for about 10 minutes until the setting point is reached.

3. Some scum will have formed on the surface, but don't worry about this – just give it a stir once off the heat and this should disperse it. Pour the liquid into warm, sterilised jars, tap them on the work surface to disperse any air bubbles and seal immediately.

Store in a cool, dark place for up to one year. Once opened, keep in the fridge and use within three months.

Straining the fruits through a muslin. This is a slow process, one drip at a time.

Damson jelly

This is a somewhat unconventional way of making fruit jelly but I have found it the best method with damsons. The fruit is frozen initially, which makes the skins split open more easily to release the juice inside. Oven-roasting damsons produces a greater quantity of liquid than boiling them on the hob; it also intensifies their flavour. This jelly is sharp and sweet all at once – a firm family favourite.

Makes approx. 1 litre (2 US pints)
—

1.5kg (3lb 5oz) frozen damsons, defrosted
600ml (1¼ US pints) water
600g (1lb 5oz) sugar

1. Pre-heat the oven to 200°c / 400°F / Gas mark 6.

2. Place the damsons (including all of the liquid released through the defrosting process) and water into a large heavy-based lidded pan (I use cast iron) and bake in the oven (with the lid on) for 50 minutes. Remove the lid and mash the damsons with a potato masher to break the fruit down some more.

3. Strain through a muslin or jelly bag into a bowl overnight. Do not squeeze the liquid through the cloth, however tempting it is.

4. Tip the damson juice into a pan and bring to the boil. Tip in the sugar and stir to dissolve. Boil rapidly for approx. 12–15 minutes until the setting point is reached.

5. Pour into warm sterilised jars and seal immediately.

Store in a cool, dark place for up to one year. Once opened, refrigerate and use within three months.

Quince membrillo

Quince is a fabulous, little-known but very British fruit, inedible raw, but aromatic and beautiful in jams and, for me, a trip down memory lane to my maternal grandmother's kitchen. You can find them in autumn in farmers' markets and greengrocers. Membrillo is a sticky, dark paste made from the pulp and is associated with Spain, Portugal and Italy. Membrillo stores well in the fridge and is great with cheese or thick yogurt. It is a lovely gift at Christmas for a cheeseboard.

Makes a large tin of Membrillo, 20cm (8 inches) square

—

2kg (4½lb) quince
300ml (1¼ cups) water
Sugar – for quantities see below

1. Roughly chop the unpeeled quinces and pop into a pan with the water. Cover and stew until fruit is soft. Sieve the fruit and measure the purée. For each 600ml (1¼ us pints) purée you'll need 350g (12½oz) of sugar.

2. Heat the purée and sugar in a wide, deep saucepan until the sugar has dissolved. Raise the heat and stir continuously to prevent catching. As it reduces it will spit, so cover your hands with a tea towel to protect them. After about 45 minutes the mixture will turn a lovely reddish-brown and will begin to come away from the sides of the pan when it is ready.

3. Pour into small baking trays lined with parchment, or for something fun, into oiled madeleine or similar trays for individual pieces. Leave to set and store wrapped in parchment in the fridge or a cool pantry.

Keeps refrigerated for six months.

Bullace cheese

Bullace are wild, small plums, purple or green, found in hedgerows and some gardens. They are sour and need more sugar than plums, so normally are not too good uncooked. Boiled up with a little sugar they are transformed. This bullace cheese is sticky and firm, lovely on a cheeseboard but also on toast or in crumbles. The rich vibrant colour will cheer you up on a wintry morning.

Makes 500ml (1 us pint)
—

1kg (2¼lb) bullace, stalks removed
150ml (⅔ cup) water
Sugar – for quantities see below

1. Put the fruit and water into a large saucepan and heat through, cooking until the stones start to rise to the top.

2. Strain the mixture through a sieve, reserving the liquid. For every 1 litre (2 us pints) of liquid weigh 500g (1lb) of sugar. Put the liquid and the sugar into a saucepan. Heat up and simmer. Once the sugar has melted keep an eye on the mixture. It will take between 25 minutes and 1 hour to reach a point where the mixture is coming away from the pan as you stir it. The cheese is ready when it has reached a lovely dark purple and, when you draw a spoon through the pan, the mixture takes its time coming together again.

3. You can pour the cheese into jars, or onto a small, lined baking tray before chopping into individual squares and wrapping in baking parchment.

Store in the fridge for up to six months.

Ruby red jam

Sometimes you have small amounts of several fruits; sometimes you just don't want a one-fruit jam. This jam is worth making whatever the reason ... a jewel of a jam, sparkling red like Dorothy's slippers in *The Wizard of Oz*.

Makes approx. 1.25 litres (2½ US pints)
—

600g (1lb 5oz) cherries
200g (7oz) strawberries, washed, hulled and halved
        or quartered depending on size
200g (7oz) redcurrants, de-stalked and checked over
800g (1¾lb) sugar

1. Heat the oven to 180°C / 350°F / Gas mark 4.

2. Pit the cherries. Put half of the pits in a muslin bag and add to the pan along with the strawberries and redcurrants. Place the sugar evenly on a baking sheet and heat on its own in the oven for 4 minutes.

3. Add the warmed sugar to the fruit, stir until dissolved and bring to a rolling boil. Boil until setting point is achieved (approx. 8–10 minutes). Remove the bag of pits. Skim off any scum that may have formed. Pour into jars and seal immediately.

Keeps for one year unopened. Once opened, refrigerate and use within three months.

Note:
You can use any combination or ratio of red fruits. Swap sour to sweet cherries, or use raspberries, cranberries or pink gooseberries. You need to think about how sweet, or not, the combination is going to be and adjust the sugar accordingly.

Black berry jam

We always have to explain the name of this jam. 'It's not "blackberry" jam, it's "black berry" jam.' Inky blue-black and fruity, it was a favourite with almost every single taste-tester that had that tough task.

Makes approx. 1.25 litres (2½ US pints)
—

600g (1lb 5oz) black raspberries
200g (7oz) blackcurrants, de-stalked
200g (7oz) mulberries, de-stalked
800g (1¾lb) sugar

1. Heat the oven to 180°C / 350°F / Gas mark 4.

2. Place all the fruit in the pan. Place the sugar evenly on a baking sheet and heat in the oven for 4 minutes. Add the warmed sugar to the fruit, stir until dissolved and bring to a rolling boil. Continue to boil for 8–10 minutes until setting point is achieved.

3. Pour into warm, sterilised jars and seal immediately.

Keeps for one year unopened. Once opened, refrigerate and use within three months.

Note:
You can use any combination of black or dark berries for this jam depending on what you like and what might be available. Other fruits might include blackberries, black raspberries, boysenberries or even elderberries. Depending on the sweetness or tartness of the kinds of berries you choose you may have to adjust the sugar amount. Make sure at least one of the berries has good pectin levels, such as currants, cranberries and gooseberries, so the jam sets easily (unless you like soft-set jam, when it is not so much of a concern).

Sour cherry jam

Sour cherries are lesser known than their sweet counterparts. They have a very short season and are also very perishable but are well worth finding and preserving so you can enjoy them for longer.

Makes 1.25 litres (2½ US pints)
—

1kg (2¼lb) sour cherries, pitted (tip: invest in a cherry or olive pitter or use a paring knife)
800g (1¾lb) sugar

1. Heat the oven to 180°C / 350°F / Gas mark 4.

2. Place the sugar evenly on a baking sheet and heat in the oven for 4 minutes. Meanwhile place the cherries in the pan. Add the warmed sugar to the fruit, stir until dissolved and bring to a rolling boil. Continue to boil for 25–30 minutes until setting point is achieved.

3. Pour into warm, sterilised jars and seal immediately.

Keeps for one year unopened. Once opened, refrigerate and use within three months.

Alternative: Sweet cherry jam
Sweet cherries are far easier to come by. To make this alternative, follow the same method as Sour cherry jam above and simply reduce the sugar quantity to 750g (1lb 6oz).

Rhubarb, strawberry and vanilla jelly

This is such a beautiful early summer jelly, a prize to reward us for making it through the winter. Forced rhubarb, as it's known in the UK, is one of the earliest things to appear in Britain but in the US rhubarb and strawberries tend to appear at the market at a similar time in late May / early June. Strawberry and rhubarb is a classic combination in jams and pies but the intensity of the colour is somehow magnified as a jelly.

Makes 750ml (1½ US pints)
—

100ml (about ½ cup) water
650g (1lb 7oz) rhubarb, cleaned, cut into 5cm (2 inch) lengths
650g (1lb 7oz) strawberries
Half a vanilla pod or 5ml (1 tsp) vanilla extract
Sugar – as required
Juice of 1 lemon

1. Put all the ingredients in a heavy-based pan with 100ml (about ½ cup) water. Simmer for about 20 minutes with the lid on, so none of the liquid evaporates, until the fruit is really soft.

2. Drain overnight or for a few hours in a jelly bag or a muslin over a bowl. Do not squeeze the bag or your jelly will be cloudy.

3. Put the drained juice in a pan and for every 1 litre (2 US pints) of liquid add 800g (1¾lb) of sugar. Add the lemon juice. Bring to a boil and continue to boil until setting point is reached, about 10 minutes.

4. Pour into sterilised jars and seal immediately.

Store in a cool, dark place for up to a year. Once opened, it should be kept refrigerated and eaten within three months.

Blueberry and lemon compote

This compote is perfect as a topping for ice cream or yogurt. I have also used it to make blueberry swirl ice cream, rather like raspberry ripple, which has become a firm favourite in the farm store over the summer.

Makes approx. 500ml (1 us pint)
—

325g (12oz) blueberries, divided into 200g and 125g
Zest of 1 lemon
100g (3½oz) sugar
75ml (⅓ cup) lemon juice (about 2 small lemons)
75ml (⅓ cup) water

SUGAR

1. Put 200g (7oz) of the blueberries in a pan along with the lemon zest, sugar and water. Heat gently until the sugar has dissolved. Increase the heat and boil for 5–8 minutes (making sure it doesn't stick on the bottom) until slightly thickened and the majority of the blueberries have burst.

2. Remove from the heat and add the lemon juice and the remaining blueberries. Fill the jars as usual and use the hot-water process for 10 minutes, following the instructions on page 78.

Store in a cool, dark place for up to a year. Once opened, refrigerate and eat within a week.

Gooseberry jelly

This jelly is a beautiful pink colour and goes really well on toast. Alternatively, you can make a slightly savoury version that goes with pork and poultry dishes (see below). It is also delicious with gooey, soft cheeses, as the slight sharpness of the jelly cuts through the richness of the cheese.

Makes approx. 2 litres (4½ us pints)
—

1.3kg (4¼lb) gooseberries, not too ripe
850ml (3½ cups) water
Sugar – as required

SUGAR

1. Heat the gooseberries and water in a covered pan over a medium heat for about 20 minutes until the gooseberries are completely soft and pulpy.

2. Strain overnight or for a few hours through a jelly bag or muslin-lined sieve and leave to drain. Do not squeeze the bag or your jelly will be cloudy.

3. When fully drained take the juice and measure it to calculate how much sugar you need. You will need 800g (1¾lb) of sugar per 1 litre (2 us pints) of juice. Put the juice in a wide heavy-bottomed pan.

4. Preheat the oven to 170°C / 325°F / Gas mark 3 and get your sterilised jars and lids warming on a baking sheet or tray. Warm the sugar in the oven for 5 minutes then add to the juice and mix to blend. Continue to stir over a medium heat until the sugar has fully dissolved. Bring to a boil and boil rapidly, stirring occasionally until setting point has been reached (start testing after about 10 minutes).

5. Once setting point has been reached remove from the heat, fill the jars, wipe the rims and seal immediately.

Keeps in a cool, dark place for up to a year. Once opened, keep refrigerated and eat within three months.

Note:
For the savoury version add 4–5 sprigs of thyme to the fruit when you cook it initially; the thyme will be removed when you drain off the juice through the jelly bag. When I fill the jars with the hot jelly, I add a small sprig of thyme to the top of each jar for decoration and a little further infusion of flavour.

You can also use the gooseberry pulp that remains after draining the juice to make a compote. Blitz it in a food processor or with a stick blender and pass it through a fine sieve, then add some elderflower cordial (shop-bought or see recipe on page 147) to the compote to sweeten and loosen it up. The amount of cordial needed will vary according to taste and consistency.

Pickled blueberries

Recipes

Vinegar

I grew up in a house full of pickle. My parents have a walk-in larder still, like an Aladdin's cave, full of delicious bottles and jars. We had an allotment when I was young and my father, now retired, still works two allotments – you can see where I got the bug from. In a more practical sense, pickling is a fabulous way to preserve bounteous harvests for enjoyment all year round. The recipes that follow are great for lunches, picnics and late-night snacks. [AD]

Vinegar has been used for many years to preserve vegetables: the science is simple. Vinegar is produced by a double fermentation of either fruit or grain. The first fermentation has yeasts turning sugar into alcohol (e.g. wine), and the second one has bacteria turning the alcohol into vinegar (or acetic acid).

Sugar (with yeasts)　　**Alcohol** (with bacteria)　　**Vinegar**

The pH level in the resulting liquid will kill any enzymes or bacteria because of its acidic nature. A pickle is therefore self-preserving and needs no refrigeration. Examples of preserving with vinegar range from pickling whole vegetables such as onions, to chutneys, relishes, mixed pickles and fresh, quick pickles.

There are many different types of vinegar used for culinary purposes, all of which can be used in pickling. Vinegar must have at least 5 per cent acidity to pickle. Most will be – but double-check the label to make sure.

Here are some vinegars we use in preserving:

Wine vinegar

Wine vinegar has a delicate flavour and colour. It is good to use when you want to retain the subtle flavour of a pickle, or the colour of golden beetroot for example. However, it is more expensive.

Malt vinegar

Dark malt vinegar has had caramel added (for colour), while distilled malt vinegar is clear. This is a strong, inexpensive vinegar, good for pickling onions and cabbage, and for bold chutneys. If you find it too strong you can always swap to a milder vinegar in a recipe if you wish.

Cider vinegar

A mild and fruity vinegar, this is lovely in chutneys, relishes and fresh pickles (or quick pickles with a shorter lifespan).

It is perfectly acceptable to use whatever vinegar you have in your kitchen without purchasing something special – better to make something with what you have than nothing at all.

It is worth noting that vinegar will react with the inside of the lids of some jars, and you may notice this when recycling jars. Look out for lids that have started to decay and discard when choosing jars and lids for preserving.

Pickled ramps, also known as wild garlic

Bread and butter (cucumber) pickles

In America, the classic bread and butter pickles (known as cucumber pickles in the UK) have a kick of heat and are sweet rather than sour. I prefer mine sourer rather than sweet because I grew up with the German version, called *senfgurken* (mustard cucumbers). This recipe combines the best of both worlds – spicy, sour and a little sweet. In place of the usual sugar I use honey.

Great eaten with cheese and cold meats as a simple lunch.

Makes approx. 1½ litres (3 US pints)

—

1kg (2¼lb) cucumbers (roughly 2 large ones)
100g (3½oz) shallots (approx. 4)
3 tsp salt
1 tsp celery seeds
2 tsp mustard seeds
½ tsp chilli flakes (optional)
1 tsp coriander seeds
4 bay leaves
1 tsp turmeric
500ml (1 US pint) cider vinegar
150ml (⅔ cup) honey

1. Peel the cucumbers and cut in half lengthways, scrape out the seeds with a spoon and discard. Slice the shallots in half and then into thin slices. Place both into a colander over a bowl, sprinkle with salt, toss with your hands and leave to drain for two hours.

2. Rinse the cucumber and shallots in cold water to remove the salt. Combine the remaining ingredients in a large saucepan and bring to the boil, stirring to dissolve the honey. Add the cucumbers and shallots, turn down the heat and cook for 5 minutes – do not allow to boil.

3. Pack into hot sterilised jars (make sure there is one bay leaf per jar) and seal immediately.

This will keep well for six months in a cool, dark place. Once opened, store in the fridge and use within two months.

Israeli pickles

Beach barbecues are what summers are made of – and we went to many growing up on the shores of Cardigan Bay. One family always used to bring pickles. These are what I remember from those summer meals. Forget the sausage in a soft white bap, forget the burger – the taste of very sharp, very crunchy, mildly spiced pickles is what I remember and loved the most.

Makes approx. 750ml (1½ US pints)
—

175g (6oz) carrots, sliced into 0.5cm (¼ inch) rounds
200g (7oz) cauliflower, cut into small bite-size chunks
300ml (1¼ cups) white wine vinegar
150ml (⅔ cup) water
1 tsp coriander seeds
½ tsp cumin seeds
2 tbsp sugar (or more to suit your tastes)
¼ tsp salt

1. Place the carrots and cauliflower into a large sterilised jar.

2. Put the vinegar, water, spices, sugar and salt into a saucepan and bring to the boil. Turn off the heat and pour over the carrots and cauliflower.

3. Seal, but allow to cool before storing in the fridge.

Store in the fridge. Keeps well for up to five weeks.

Pickled peaches

Pickled peaches are typical fare in the southern US states. During peak season, stands line the roadside with jars of 'Nana's pickled peaches'. Traditionally they are eaten alongside a hot pork roast but I enjoy them just as much with cold meats and pâtés, or even in a sandwich. I find it best to use slightly under-ripe fruit for this recipe: that way they stay firmer for longer when stored.

Makes approx. 2 litres (4 US pints)
—

225g (8oz) demerara sugar (US turbinado sugar)
10 cloves
1 small cinnamon stick
4cm (1¾ inch) piece fresh ginger, peeled and sliced
500ml (1 US pint) white wine vinegar
2kg (4½lb) ripe peaches

1. Place the sugar, cloves, cinnamon, ginger and vinegar in a large saucepan and bring to the boil, stirring occasionally to dissolve the sugar. Turn off the heat and set aside.

2. Using a sharp knife, lightly score the peaches with a cross at the base. Place the peaches in a large saucepan and cover with just-boiled water. Allow to stand for 3 minutes. Remove with a slotted spoon and plunge into ice-cold water to stop them cooking further. Now the skins should be easy to remove with a paring knife, starting at the marked cross.

3. Once the peaches are peeled, remove the stone and cut them into 8 wedges.

4. Bring the vinegar mixture back up to a boil, add the peaches, turn down the heat and simmer for about

15 minutes without a lid until the fruit is tender but still holds it's shape well.

5. Spoon the peaches into warm, sterilised jars, pour over the hot vinegar to cover the fruit completely and seal immediately with vinegar-proof lids.

Store in a cool, dark place. If you can, keep for at least one month before eating as the flavour intensifies over time, just like a chutney does. These peaches will keep well for up to one year. Once opened, refrigerate and eat within three months.

Watermelon rind pickles

What I love about this recipe is that it uses a part of the fruit which I believe most people would discard and deem inedible, and turns it into a deliciously tangy and most versatile pickle. Watermelon rind is not particularly flavoursome, but this works in its favour as it means it takes on the warm flavours of the spices.

Makes approx. 750ml (1½ US pints)
—

For the brine
1 litre (4 cups) water
100g (3½oz) salt
For the pickle
1kg (2¼lb) watermelon rind
250g (9oz) sugar
250ml (1 cup) cider vinegar
1 small cinnamon stick
5 cloves

1. Mix the water and salt together in a large bowl until all the granules have dissolved.

2. Peel the watermelon rind and get rid of any red bits of flesh – you just want the whitish/greenish rind here. Cut the rind into roughly 3cm × 1cm (1½ × ½ inch) strips.

3. Place the watermelon rind into the brine, ensuring the pieces are all covered, and soak overnight. Drain rind and rinse in cold water to get rid of the salt. Cover with fresh water and boil for 20 minutes until tender.

4. In a large saucepan heat the sugar, vinegar and spices, stirring to dissolve the sugar. Once boiling, turn down the heat, add the watermelon rind and simmer for 15–20 minutes until the rind becomes translucent.

5. Take off the heat, pack into hot sterilised jars ensuring that the rind is completely covered by liquid and seal immediately.

Keeps well for up to one year in a cool, dark place. The rind will become softer over time, so for a crunchy pickle eat before six months. Once opened, store in the fridge and eat within two months.

Sweet pepper relish

This relish is about as simple as it gets to make. It's sweet and tangy and the perfect accompaniment to sausages and barbecued foods.

Makes 1¼ litres (2½ US pints)
—

500g (1lb 2oz) red bell peppers (about 3), deseeded and chopped finely
500g (1lb 2oz) green bell peppers (about 3), deseeded and chopped finely
1 large white onion, peeled and chopped finely
375ml (1½ cups) cider vinegar
8 tbsp sugar
1½ tsp yellow mustard seeds
1 tsp celery seeds
½ tsp turmeric
1½ tsp salt

1. Place all the ingredients into a pan, bring to the boil, stir to dissolve the sugar. Turn the heat down, cover and simmer for 20 minutes.

2. Pack into sterilised jars while still hot and seal immediately.

Store in a cool, dark place. Keeps well for up to one year. Once opened, store in the fridge and eat within two months.

VINEGAR

Courgette (zucchini) relish

Most people I know who have a garden get a week or two during the summer where things just go BOOM. Courgettes seem to be one of those things that come in abundance all at once. This is a great recipe for using up any gluts and also works well with marrows in place of courgette. I like my relish to be chunky so I dice the vegetables, but you could grate them or pulse them in a food processor if you prefer a finer texture.

Makes approx. 1¾ litres (3¾ US pints)
—

1kg (2¼lb) courgettes, diced finely
1 large onion, diced finely
1 tsp salt
500g (1lb) green bell peppers, diced finely
750ml (3 cups) apple cider vinegar
150g (5oz) light brown sugar
1 tsp turmeric
2 tsp celery seeds

1. Place the courgettes and onion into a colander, sprinkle with salt, mix with your hands and stand them over a bowl for an hour to drain off some of the excess liquid. There is no need to rinse the salt off after draining.

2. Combine all the ingredients in a large saucepan and bring to the boil, stirring occasionally to dissolve the sugar. Once boiling, turn down the heat and simmer for 30 minutes.

3. Ladle the relish, boiling hot, into hot sterilised jars, tap down on the work surface to bring any air bubbles up to the surface and seal immediately.

Store in a cool, dark place. Keeps well for up to one year. Once opened, store in the fridge and eat within two months.

Pickled blueberries

The addition of cinnamon in these pickles is inspired by the classic all-American blueberry pie. They are perfect in a Brie sandwich or simply served alongside cold meats and cheese. Blackberries can be pickled in exactly the same way. They have a sharper flavour and so may require a little more sugar according to taste.

Makes approx. 400ml (¾ US pint)
—

100ml (about ½ cup) white wine vinegar
50ml (¼ cup) water
50g (2oz) sugar
¼ tsp salt
150g (5oz) blueberries
1 small cinnamon stick

1. In a small saucepan heat the vinegar, water, sugar and salt until all the granules have dissolved. Set the vinegar mixture aside and allow to cool.

2. Put the blueberries and cinnamon stick into a sterilised jar and pour the vinegar mixture over. Cover and leave in the fridge for a day before using. The pickles intensify in flavour the longer they are kept.

These keep for up to four weeks in the fridge. For recipe photograph, see pages 44–45.

Pear, lemon and ginger chutney

This is a fruity chutney with a delicate warmth from the ginger. It is an onion-free recipe, which allows the pear to shine. Very ripe, soft pears should ideally be used for this chutney, but I have used hard pears before and they work fine. However, they will need mashing with a potato masher at the very end to break the flesh down a little.

Makes approx. 1.5 litres (3 US pints)
—

3 lemons, finely sliced, seeds discarded
2kg (4½lb) ripe pears
175g (6oz) raisins
50g (2oz) piece of ginger, peeled and grated finely
400ml (1¾ cups) cider vinegar
300g (11oz) light brown sugar
½ tsp ground cloves
1 tsp ground cinnamon

1. Chop the lemon slices into small bits, place them in a small pan, cover with cold water and bring to the boil. Once boiled, discard the water and cover with fresh cold water. Bring to the boil again and simmer for 10–15 minutes, by which time all the bitterness should have come out of the lemons and the rind should be soft. Drain off the water.

2. Place all the ingredients (including the lemon) in a large pan and slowly bring the mixture to the boil, stirring from time to time. Simmer for about 2 hours. It is ready when a spoon dragged along the bottom of the pan leaves a clear streak (i.e. the vinegar doesn't run back in straight away).

3. Pack the hot chutney into sterilised jars and seal.

Store in a cool, dark place. This chutney needs to mature a little in the jar, so I would suggest keeping it for three months before opening. Keeps well for up to two years. Once opened, store in the fridge and use within three months.

Sweet pickled mushrooms with thyme

I am a huge fan of mushrooms any way they come, but these are particularly special – they lift a meal from the humdrum to the extraordinary. These are perfect on their own as a pickle alongside meats and cheeses but I like to use them as a 'topper' for soups and stews. They go very well with lentils and pulses.

Makes approx. 1 litre (2 US pints)
—

500ml (1 US pint) white wine vinegar
175ml (¾ cup) runny honey
1 tsp salt
500g (1lb 2oz) mushrooms, cut into 1cm (½ inch) slices
        (any variety – button mushrooms work well)
2 large sprigs thyme
2 cloves garlic, peeled and sliced
2 bay leaves
5 shallots, thinly sliced (optional)
4 strips of lemon zest

1. Put the vinegar, honey and salt in a saucepan and bring to a boil over a medium heat, stirring occasionally so the honey mixes in and the salt dissolves. Turn off the heat and set to one side.

2. Divide the mushrooms, thyme, garlic, bay, shallots and lemon zest equally between two sterilised jars and pour the hot vinegar mixture over the top, ensuring everything is completely covered, and seal.

Store in the fridge. Unopened these should keep for up to two months. Once opened, eat within three weeks.

Pickling vinegar

You can make up a bottle of this vinegar for a particular recipe you are following, and keep any left over for another time. It is used in the next few recipes and is good to use as an all-round vinegar. Often pickling is not an exact science: it depends on the size and shape of what you are preserving. I often have some in the kitchen for when I want to make a little jar of something. Make sure you label it properly though, or you might end up with pickling vinegar in your salad dressing!

Makes approx. 1 litre (2 US pints)
—

1 litre (2 US pints) vinegar –
    white wine is good for nasturtium seeds,
    malt is good for pickling onions and beetroot,
    cider vinegar is good for eggs, or when you want to
    really see the colour of the thing you are pickling
    (in general, any will do, and you can also mix vinegars)
1 garlic clove
1 tsp peppercorns
1 tsp black mustard seeds
6 juniper berries
6 whole cardamom pods
1 dried red chilli

1. Place all the ingredients in the pan and bring to the boil for 10 minutes, allow to cool thoroughly, then sieve.

2. Pour back into bottle and use immediately – or store until needed. You can play around with the amount of chilli – I add more for pickled onions and beetroot.

Store in a cool, dark place. Will keep for one year.

Pickled onions

When I left home my father gave me a large glass jar, like the types you used to see in sweet shops, full of pickled onions. It would be replenished each year as long as it was returned.

Makes 800ml (1¾ us pints)
—

500g (1lb 2oz) pickling onions
400ml (1¾ cups) pickling malt vinegar, see page 61
100g (3½oz) fine salt

1. Peel the onions. This is painful at the best of times – especially if you are doing a few kilos. One way is to peel them in water, so fill a bowl with water and place all the onions in and peel holding the onion under the surface (we used to get roped in as children to help out with this).

2. Pat the onions dry as you peel and place in a large bowl, sprinkling liberally with salt as you go. Leave overnight.

3. Rinse the salt off and pour away any liquid, pat the onions dry. Place the onions in a sterilized bottle – it will depend on their shape and size how many will fit – and cover with pickling vinegar.

These will be ready in six weeks and will keep for a year in a cool, dark place.

Alternative: Pickled red cabbage
Delicious with cheese and in sandwiches, a glorious riot of colour on the plate to cheer you up at any time of year.

Follow the recipe above, using one large red cabbage sliced finely. You only need to leave it covered in salt for a couple of hours before putting it into jars and covering with vinegar. It is good to use a light vinegar here, like cider or white wine, or even white malt vinegar.

Pickled beetroot

Any beetroot will do here, though the purple will leach and cancel out the other colours, so you could just pickle golden and stripy beetroot together, or mix them all up. This is fabulous in a Cheddar sandwich, but lovely for a 'picnic' lunch as we call it in our house, with cheese, cured meats and fish, salads, bread and butter, and pickles for everyone to tuck into.

Makes 800ml (1¾ US pints)
—

500g (1lb 2oz) purple and golden beetroot (if you can get it)
350ml (¾ US pint) pickling malt vinegar, see page 61
1 dried chilli – optional

1. Cook the beetroot whole if small, chop into similar-sized pieces if large, and boil for 30–60 minutes until tender, then allow to cool completely.

2. Pop into jars and cover with vinegar – you could add a dried chilli here if you like things spicy.

Ready after one month, and it will keep in a cool, dark place for six months.

Alternative: Golden pickled beetroot with thyme and chilli
Follow the recipe above but use only golden beetroot, then make the pickling vinegar with cider vinegar. This way you can see the beautiful colour of the beetroot. When placing the beetroot and vinegar in the jar add a sprig or two of fresh thyme and a couple of dried chillis.

Pickled nasturtium seeds

On the smallholding, we are always trying to find a way to create preserves that will bring our food to life in the winter months. Nasturtium leaves and flowers are peppery and delicious in salads, and the seeds pickle well and can be used in place of capers. I would suggest making up a large bottle of the pickling vinegar for this and then make a small jar each week when the nasturtium flowers are in season.

Makes 200ml (approx. ½ US pint)
—

Some freshly picked nasturtium seeds – two handfuls is enough
100g (3½oz) salt – large crystals if you can get them but sea salt is fine
200ml (¾ cup) spiced pickling vinegar, see page 61

1. Pick the nasturtium seeds when still green, gathering enough to fill a small jam jar.

2. Place seeds in a bowl and cover them in salt for 24 hours. Strain and rinse off salt and pat dry. Pop in jar and cover with vinegar.

They keep well for eight months. Once opened, keep in the fridge and eat within four weeks. (See also recipe for salted nasturtiums on page 108.)

Rhubarb and turmeric pickle

I love the typically Indian oily pickles eaten with curries, but they are also great with cold meats, cheese and in a sandwich; they can bring a simple dish alive. This recipe was given to me by a dear local friend, Martin, who loves a good curry. He adapted it from a recipe by New Zealand food writer Digby Law.

Makes 800ml (1¾ us pints)
—

750g (1½lb) rhubarb
½ tbsp dried red chillis
½ tbsp ground turmeric
25g (1oz) ginger, grated
5 garlic cloves, grated
110ml (½ cup) vegetable oil
1 tsp each of fenugreek, cumin and mustard seeds
2 curry leaves
4 fresh green chillis, chopped finely
450ml (2 cups) white malt vinegar – you might not use it all
1 tbsp salt

1. Slice the rhubarb into chunks. Grind the dried chillis, turmeric, ginger and garlic into a paste. Heat the oil in a large pan and fry the paste for 5 minutes.

2. Add all the seeds and curry leaves and cook for 2 minutes, then add the rhubarb and green chillis.

3. Pour just enough vinegar to almost cover. Add salt and simmer until rhubarb is tender.

4. Pour into sterilised jars.

Keeps for a year. Once opened, store in the refrigerator and use within three months.

Green tomato chutney

My favourite recipe of all. I wrote this down when leaving home to go to university aged 18. When I was 40 my mother decided I was ready to have her secret recipe – little did she know I'd been making it for the last 20 years! Any recipe that uses something no longer edible in the normal sense is a bonus when you grow your own. This is delicious with curry or with cheese, and great in sandwiches.

Makes 1.2 litres (2½ us pints)

—

3cm (1¼ inches) root ginger, grated
15 cloves garlic, grated
1½–2 tsp garam masala
1½–2 tsp chilli powder
500g (1lb) brown sugar
1 kg (2¼lb) green tomatoes, halved if small, chopped up
**   if large**
350ml (1½ cups) malt vinegar

1. Put everything into a wide pan, dissolve the sugar and bring to the boil. Cook for 50–55 minutes until thick.

2. Bottle while hot. You can alter the amount of chilli to taste.

Keeps for two years and longer. Once opened, use within three months.

Left to right
Pickled beetroot, Green tomato chutney
and Pickled onions

Young ramps, also known as wild garlic

Pickled ramps

Ramps, or wild garlic, are one of the first signs of growth and life after winter. They grow in shaded wooded areas, often near streams, and are a forager's treasure. When foraging for them, or anything else for that matter, it is very important to make sure you leave enough for healthy regrowth. The general rule of thumb is to take less than one-third of the plant or crop. Ramps regrow from their bulb, so if you take the bulbs as well as the leaves they will not grow back ... ever. This recipe calls for both leaves and bulbs, so for that reason make only a few precious jars and do something else like ramp kimchi (see page 109) that uses only the leaves for more rampy goodness.

Makes 225g (½ us pint)
—

120ml (½ cup) white wine vinegar
40ml (8 tsp) water
1 tsp sugar
¼ tsp salt
50g (2oz) ramps (bulbs and stalks)
¼ tsp pink peppercorns
¼ tsp yellow mustard seeds

1. Gently heat the white wine vinegar, water, sugar and salt in a small saucepan until the sugar and salt have dissolved completely.

2. Place the ramps in a sterilised jar (I prefer root end down) and pour the hot liquid over the ramps. Sprinkle the peppercorns and mustard seeds into the jar so they are as evenly spread as possible.

3. Seal the jar and leave for a week.

Keep for up to a year. Once opened, keep refrigerated and use within three months. For recipe photograph see page 49.

Hot and thick tomato sauce

This is one of those super spicy sauces that tastes delicious in a wrap with barbecued meat or veg and minty yogurt, the beautiful trinity. A good sauce will bring a dish alive, and this one certainly fits the bill.

Makes 500ml (1 us pint)
—

500g (1lb 2oz) tomatoes, any type and size, peeled and chopped into bite-size pieces
1 tsp ground cumin
1 tsp ground coriander
½–1 tsp cayenne, to taste
100g (3½oz) soft brown sugar
100ml (about ½ cup) cider vinegar
1 tsp salt
2 cloves finely grated garlic
2cm (1 inch) finely grated ginger

1. To peel a tomato, make a cross with a knife at the base of the tomato then place it in boiling water for a maximum of one minute (any longer and the tomato flesh will start to disintegrate). The skin will start to split, take it out and peel (large tomatoes are easier to peel). As you work through the tomatoes you will need to replenish the boiling water.

2. Place all the ingredients into a saucepan and cook for 1½ hours until the sauce is dark and sticky.

This is ready to eat straight away. Refrigerate and it will last for one month.

Chilli ketchup

I have a ketchup confession to make – I'm really not a fan, so much so that I'm often the butt of ketchup jokes. However, if you give me a real ketchup, with some care taken when making, then I am rather partial to it. This chilli ketchup is delicious on chips, with eggs, or in a bun with some pulled pork or beef. Apples come into season at the end of the tomato season, so this is a great way of using up old battered tomatoes and the windfall apples. You can leave the chilli out altogether, or add more to taste.

Makes 500ml (1 US pint)

—

500g (1lb 2oz) chopped tomatoes (these can be really ripe)
125g (4½oz) finely chopped red onions
125g (4½ oz) chopped and peeled windfall apples
6 fresh chopped chillis (or to taste)
120ml (½ cup) white wine vinegar
2 tsp salt
3 tsp smoked paprika
120g (4¼oz) dark brown sugar

1. Put all ingredients except the sugar into a pan and cook slowly for 1½–2 hours until starting to thicken. Carefully blend using either a stick blender or by transferring the mixture into a blender. Once smooth, pour back into the pan and bring up to a high temperature, then simmer.

2. Add the sugar and cook until the mixture thickens – you will need to stir all the time.

3. Bottle and refrigerate.

Once opened, use within three weeks.

VINEGAR

Recipes

BOTTLING

Bottling

Bottling, canning or 'hot-water bath processing' needs to be done when the contents of the jar are either low-acid or when fruit or vegetables are being bottled as 'themselves', i.e. not preserved by using any of the other methods (sugar, salt, oil and so on); anything where the contents are not being further preserved by making their environment inhospitable to pathogens. Examples of foods that require the bottling process are fruit in juice or syrup, asparagus, beans or tomato sauce, passata or plain tomatoes.

Bottling can seem intimidating but it needn't be. It's simple once you know the basics and if you use common sense. There are some rules but none of them are complicated and as long as you follow the steps methodically you should have no problems.

In the US it is generally recommended that all jarred preserves are processed by this method to be sure to kill all pathogens, but in the UK this is not the case. In the UK jams, jellies and chutneys are not typically hot-water processed. The recipes in this chapter require it. For the other recipes in the book it is up to you whether you do it or not.

Filling hot sterilised jars using
a ladle and wide-mouthed funnel

The Equipment

The equipment necessary is not expensive or complicated and can make the whole process a lot easier, so if you plan to make preserves that require this method of preserving, it's worth purchasing as much as you can afford.

Containers
These are typically jars or bottles with special lids, such as Kilner, Weck or Le Parfait jars that have rubber gaskets and metal clips, or Ball or Mason jars that have metal lids and rings. The jars don't have to be brand new but they do need to be free of any imperfections such as chips or cracks. However, the lids and the gaskets do need to be new each time you bottle something in them. This is to ensure a complete seal. There is also a slight chance they might explode under the pressure of boiling if they are cracked, chipped or used too many times (it sounds scary but is likely to be more messy than dangerous – think tomato passata all over your kitchen walls!)

Pans
You can buy large enamel pans with metal racks to keep the jars off the bottom of the pan relatively cheaply. You could also place a rack in the bottom of a large stock pot with a lid (the jars should not directly touch the bottom of the pan). The pan needs to be deep enough to contain your filled jars submerged by an extra inch or two of boiling water.

Baking sheets
Use these or trays with clean tea towels or dish cloths on them to hold the warm clean jars and lids that have been through the hot-water bath and are sitting to settle and cool.

Other useful equipment

— **A jar lifter** that makes taking hot, heavy jars out of boiling water much easier
— **A pair of long tongs** (or a magnetic 'lid lifter') for getting lids, rings and gaskets out of boiling water
— **A jar-filling (wide-mouth) funnel** to make pouring chunky liquids easier and neater

The Method

As with any method of preserving, your jars and lids need to be scrupulously clean when you fill them with your delicious preserves so that nothing can contaminate them from within. This can be done in one of several ways:

— the sanitising cycle on your dishwasher
— by submerging in boiling water for at least 10 minutes
— by heating in a 140°C / 280°F / Gas mark 1 oven for 20 minutes

The jars need to be warm or hot when you fill them so I find the easiest option is to time it so they come out of the dishwasher when the preserve is ready to be put into jars. If that doesn't work out then I already have the canning pot full of boiling water on the stove top, so the clean empty jars can go straight into that water. I hold them there and remove them as I am ready to fill them.

When you are ready to fill the jars, take them out of the boiling water (dishwasher or oven) and place them on a nearby baking tray. Take out the lids and have them draining on a clean cloth nearby. Don't dry them with a tea towel. The heat will cause any remaining water to evaporate.

Then, using the funnel, pour in your preserves and fill to within 6–12mm (¼–½ inch) of the top, i.e. the space between the top of the preserve and the underside of the lid. The smaller gap is for jams and jellies, the larger gap for whole fruits, apple compote and tomatoes. This allows for an airspace that will expand and contract as the jars go through the bottling process. If the space is too small food will be forced out of the lid. While the jars are in the boiling water, the air in this headspace is pushed out of the jar. Then, when the jar comes out of the hot water, the air contracts, sucking the gasket or lid on to the jar rim to create a vacuum seal. If the space is not large enough or too large this seal doesn't happen and the food will not be preserved any longer than normal food safety limits would dictate.

Once filled, wipe the rims of the jars with a damp paper towel or clean cloth to ensure there is nothing that will prevent a good seal.

Put on the lids and rings and tighten fingertip tight – not too tight, as the air needs to escape in the first instance. If using jars with rubber gaskets, simply close the jars with the metal clamp. They are designed to release the air themselves.

Carefully transfer the jars to the canning pot, being careful not to knock them causing them to fall over or crack. The filled jars need to remain upright for the air to escape fully and the seal to complete properly. I often add empty jars to the pan to fill it and help stabilise the other jars. Make sure the water is at least 2.5cm (1 inch) above the tallest jar; if not, top up with boiling water.

Raise the heat so the water is boiling rapidly and start the timer. You need to ensure that the jars are in the boiling water for the amount of time required by each individual recipe, or sterilisation will not be complete. Going over the time will not inherently do any damage but it might affect the flavour and texture slightly.

When the correct time has elapsed, turn off the heat and remove the jars carefully onto a baking sheet or tray covered in a clean cloth. As soon as you take the jars out of the pan some of them will start 'popping'. This is the air in the airspace contracting and sucking the lid back onto the jar rim, completing the sealing process. Some will take a few more minutes than others.

After about an hour you should check the seals on all your jars. With the ring and lid jars you can press on the dimple in the lid – if the dimple pops then the seal is not complete and you should go through the process again or eat the contents within a week. If the dimple seems to be 'down' and fixed you can further check by removing the ring and trying to lift the jar by just the lid. If you can do this, you have achieved a complete seal.

If you are using the jars with rubber gaskets, you can check them by opening/removing the metal clasp/clips and trying to lift the jar by the glass lid. If you can lift without the jar opening then you have also achieved a complete seal.

Once you have established the seals are good then you need to leave the jars on the baking tray for a further 11 or so hours to settle and cool undisturbed. Any jars that are not sealed should be reprocessed as soon as possible. This is done by removing the lids/gaskets and replacing with new ones after checking that there were no other reasons for not sealing such as stray food on the jar rim or a crack or chip in the rim. You can then reprocess with new lids or gaskets and hopefully it will work second time around.

The processed, checked and cooled jars should be kept somewhere dark and cool until you break into them to eat the contents! Sunlight will cause the contents to deteriorate. Once they are opened, how soon they need to be eaten depends on what they contain. Typically I would eat them within the time range I would had they not been sterilised, as once they are open they are, by definition, no longer sterile. Always using a clean utensil to get the contents out of an opened jar will ensure they remain uncontaminated.

This is where common sense comes in. If, when you open them or before, something looks amiss, such as the presence of mould, the lid is bulging or when you open it there is a fizzing sound or a weird smell, then discard the contents safely and immediately. Try not to weep! Make sure the contents cannot be consumed by anything accidentally. Contamination with botulism is very rare; however, it is a small but serious risk when bottling / canning, mainly with low-acid items. If in doubt, don't taste it to check, just dispose of the whole jar and its contents.

Check each recipe carefully to make sure you process your preserves for the correct amount of time. One thing to note if you are processing at altitude is that higher altitudes require longer processing times. Just follow these guidelines:

Altitude	Canning time adjustment
305–915m (1,001–3,000ft)	+5 minutes
916–1825m (3,001–6,000ft)	+10 minutes
1826–2435m (6,001–8,000ft)	+15 minutes
2436–3050m (8,001–10,000ft)	+20 minutes

Top
Boiling until setting point
is reached
Bottom
Filling hot sterilised jars

Top
Placing lids and rings on filled jars once the rims have been wiped clean
Bottom
Placing jars into the hot-water bath using a jar lifter

Aubergine (Eggplant) sauce

This sauce is a very valuable jar to have in the larder – it is ready for any occasion, whether it be a quiet family dinner or a party with friends. Great with pasta or rice, alongside grilled meats or used as a crostini topping.

Makes approx. 1.75 litres (3½ US pints)
—

2 (approx. 1kg / 2¼lb) large aubergines (eggplant), diced into large chunks
1 (220g/8oz) large red pepper, diced
8 cloves garlic, peeled
12 (1.2kg/2½lb) tomatoes, quartered
5 sprigs of marjoram
2 tsp salt
½ tsp freshly ground black pepper
60ml (4 tbsp) olive oil
45ml (3 tbsp) balsamic vinegar
15ml (1 tbsp) lemon juice (approx. juice of ¼ lemon)
Sugar to taste (optional)

1. Heat the oven to 250°C / 475°F / Gas mark 9.

2. Lay the aubergine, pepper, garlic, tomatoes and marjoram on a large baking tray. Sprinkle with salt and pepper, then drizzle with the oil and balsamic vinegar. Use your hands to mix everything together thoroughly. Place the tray in the centre of the oven and roast for 50–60 minutes – turning halfway through – until some of the vegetables are beginning to char around the edges (this is where the flavour comes from).

3. Put the vegetables into a food processor (this may have to be done in two batches) and blitz until smooth. Transfer the aubergine sauce to a large pan, squeeze

over the lemon juice and stir. Taste and adjust with a little sugar / salt / pepper if needed.

4. Pour the sauce into sterilised jars, tap them on the work surface to dispel any air bubbles and loosely seal according to jar type. Process in a hot-water canner (see page 78) for 35 minutes. Lay a tea towel on the work surface, place the jars upright onto this and leave to cool. Test the seals (see page 80) and, if OK, tighten and store until ready to use.

Store in a cool, dark place. Keeps well for up to a year. Once opened, refrigerate and use within five days.

Spiced apple, pear and prune compote

This is comfort food in its purest form. It is one of the first things I fed my children but it is by no means baby food. Delicious with custard, yogurt or simply on its own – it makes for a perfect winter breakfast or dessert. I eat it by the bowlful.

Makes approx.3 litres (6 us pints)
—

Juice of half a lemon (to prevent oxidisation)
1.5kg (3lb 6oz) eating apples (about 9 apples, any variety)
3kg (6lb 12oz) pears (about 21 pears, any variety)
120ml (½ cup) lemon juice (roughly 2 lemons)
24 prunes
2 cinnamon sticks, each 5cm (2 inches) in length
18 cloves (in a herb bag)
¾ tsp grated nutmeg

1. To avoid the fruit oxidising and turning brown, I always have a large bowl half-full of cold water with half a lemon squeezed in at the side of the chopping board.

2. Peel and core the apples, popping them into the bowl of water as you go. Do the same with the pears. Working quickly, dice the apples and pears into 2cm (1 inch) chunks and put them into a large saucepan, then pour over the lemon juice. Add the prunes, cinnamon sticks, cloves and nutmeg. Give everything a stir.

3. Cover and stew over a medium heat for about 20 minutes until the apples and pears are falling apart. Stir from time to time to avoid sticking at the base of the pan or burning.

4. Once the fruit has turned into a mush, remove the cinnamon sticks and clove bag. Pour the mixture into a food processor (this may need to be done in two batches) and blitz to a smooth purée.

5. Pour the compote into sterilised jars and tap on the work surface to remove any air bubbles. Screw the lids onto the jars and process in a hot-water canner for 15 minutes. Cover the work surface with a tea towel, remove the jars and place on top. Let them sit undisturbed until cool. Test the seals and, if good, screw the lid tightly on or clip the jars shut.

Store in a cool, dark place for up to a year. Once opened, refrigerate and eat within five days.

Bottled mulberries

Mulberries are similar to blackberries in appearance but, depending on the variety, can be much less sharp or far more intense in flavour. In Northeast America the first mulberries are out at the start of July, but in the UK they appear in late August / September. This recipe can easily be halved. Mulberries have small green stalks but if you prefer snip them off with scissors.

Makes approx. 2 litres (4 US pints)
—

1kg (2¼lb) mulberries
4 strips of lemon zest
For the syrup
1 litre (2 US pints) water
200g (7oz) granulated sugar

1. To make the syrup combine the sugar and water in a saucepan and bring to the boil over a medium heat, stirring to dissolve the sugar granules.

2. Pack the mulberries tightly into the sterilised jars. Push a strip of lemon zest down the side of each jar.

3. Pour the warm syrup over the mulberries.

4. Seal the jars up and process in a hot-water canner for 15 minutes.

5. Remove the jars and place them upright on the work surface. Tighten the screw bands immediately and allow to cool. Once cool check the seals.

Store in a cool, dark place for up to a year. Once opened, store in the fridge and use within five days.

Apple and ginger compote

I have been making apple compote since I became a mother and I love it now as much as the children did back then. I make all sorts of variations but this one with ginger is really good. A little zing of heat from the ginger makes it a bit more interesting than just plain apple sauce. As with any apple compote it can be used in so many ways: on its own, as a topping for yogurt, cereal or pancakes, or as the base for a crumble. It is so nice to have a few jars of this somewhere safe so you can pull one out to dip into anytime you feel like it. It's my fruit of choice during the winter and is one of the many useful ways to preserve a surplus of apples should you have one.

Makes 1 litre (2 us pints)
—

1kg (2¼lb) apples, any kind you have or a mixture, peeled and cored
3cm (1¼ inches) ginger, peeled and grated
Zest and juice of half an orange

1. Chop the apples roughly and put in a large heavy-based pan. Add the ginger, the orange zest and juice and a splash of water and put the lid on the pan. Have sterilised jars and lids warming along with your hot-water canner.

2. Warm over a medium-high heat then reduce to medium-low once the water and juice in the bottom is bubbling. Continue to simmer until the apples are soft. Some apples, depending on the variety, will mush right down while others will retain their shape. It doesn't matter which ones you have, just cook until they are soft.

3. Blitz* the apple sauce until smooth. I use a hand-held (stick or immersion) blender but you can use a food processor or a food mill if you prefer.

4. Fill the warm jars and tap on the work surface to remove any air bubbles. Put lids on and tighten to finger-tight.

5. Process in the hot-water canner for 15 minutes for 500ml jars (1 US pint), 20 minutes for 1 litre (2 US pints). Remove and let sit for 12 hours, checking the jar seal after about an hour.

Keeps for a year unopened. Refrigerate and use within five days once opened.

* *You don't have to blitz the sauce if you prefer it very chunky, and also you can blitz in varying degrees so you can have chunkier or less chunky, as you prefer.*

Peach sauce

This is a soft-set jam that I discovered by accident one day when first trying to make peach jam. I just added the sugar to the fruit and tried to make jam using my usual method. Peaches, however, have less pectin and a higher water content than some fruit and therefore once the jam had cooked it was still quite runny. I tried it and discovered it was actually perfect to have on top of yogurt for breakfast or, of course, ice cream. Now I often make this and peach jam 'proper' – although this works equally well on toast, it's just a little messier to eat!

Makes approx. 2.5 litres (5 US pints)
—

1.8kg (4lb) peaches
2.6kg (3lb 3oz) sugar
Juice of half a lemon

1. Heat the oven to 170°C / 325°F / Gas mark 3, and put a couple of small plates in your freezer to cool.

2. *Optional step* – peeling the peaches. Heat a pan of water to boiling and mark each peach with a cross with a knife and put a few in the pan at a time and leave for about a minute. Remove and place in a bowl of cold water to cool and continue until you have done all of them. Drain and peel.

3. Place the sugar on a sided baking tray and heat for about 4–6 minutes until warm.

4. Cut each peach into pieces of around 1cm dice (½ inch). (Sometimes I cut them bigger as I quite like it chunky, it's up to you.) Put the peaches in a wide, heavy-bottomed pan along with the lemon juice and add the sugar once heated.

5. Bring to a boil, stirring to help dissolve the sugar. Boil while stirring occasionally for 5 minutes. Turn off the heat and test for set. I want this to be a soft set as I want it to remain runny so it can be used as part jam, part topping. If it is not ready then return it to the heat for 2–3 minutes more and repeat the set test.

6. Once you have the set you like then fill the warm sterilised jars, wipe the rims and put on the lids finger-tip tight.

7. Process in a hot-water canner for 10 minutes and remove and allow to sit for 12 hours or overnight, after testing that the lids are correctly sealed.

Store in a cool, dark place for up to a year. Once opened, refrigerate and consume within three months.

Peach and mulberry compote

Pure sunshine in a jar – without wanting to sound clichéd.

Makes 1.5 litres (3 US pints)

—

1kg (2¼lb) peaches, peeled, de-stoned and roughly chopped
500g (1lb 2oz) mulberries
30ml (2 tbsp) lemon juice (approx. juice of half a lemon)
Honey (optional)

1. Place the peaches, mulberries and lemon juice into a saucepan. Pop the lid on and simmer over a medium heat for about 15 minutes or until the peaches are soft and falling apart. Stir from time to time to avoid sticking and burning.

2. Once the fruit has turned into a mush, test for sweetness. If you prefer a sweeter compote, add some honey (a tablespoon at a time), and stir so that everything is well mixed. Test for sweet / sour balance and repeat until the desired sweetness is achieved.

3. Pour the compote into sterilised jars and tap on the work surface to disperse any air bubbles. Seal and process in a hot-water canner for 20 minutes. Cover the work surface with a tea towel, remove the jars and place on top of the towel. Let these sit undisturbed until cool. Test the seals and, if good, screw the lid tightly on.

Store in a cool, dark place for up to a year. Once opened, store in the fridge and consume within five days.

BOTTLING

Pear and apple maple butter

This butter epitomises autumn, making the most of the fruits of the season. It doesn't yield much but it's well worth making a jar or two as an indulgence or as a special gift for someone. Use it to spread on toast or to sandwich two cakes together.

Makes 1.25 litres (2½ US pints)
—

2kg (4½lb) pears (approx. 12–14)
1.6kg (3½lb) eating apples (approx. 6)
12 cloves
250ml (1 cup) water
120ml (½ cup) maple syrup
60g (2oz) sugar

1. Chop up the pears and apples (no need to peel or core) and add to a large pan along with all the other ingredients. Heat to a boil and then simmer gently in a covered pan until the fruit is completely cooked through and very soft (about 15 minutes).

2. Push the fruits through a fine-to-medium sieve.

3. Put the fruits into a wide pan and add the maple syrup and sugar. Heat gently and allow to cook on the lowest burner setting for about 2½–3 hours, stirring occasionally to be sure it doesn't catch on the bottom of the pan. Be more and more careful as the mixture gets thicker and thicker.

4. When thick and reduced to a spreadable consistency, pour the reduced liquid into clean sterilised jars, making sure to get rid of any air bubbles. Put on the lids and rings and hot-water process for 15 minutes, checking the seal as usual.

Store in a cool, dark place for up to a year. Once opened, refrigerate and consume within one month.

Bottled cherries

Cherry season seems so fleeting … they are suddenly here and then they are gone, like so many fruits we wait for each year. I can't eat enough cherries in that short time to keep me satisfied until the following year. Bottling them allows you to extend the season a little longer or indeed give you a blast of cheering cherry in the depths of winter. They go really well with game and, of course, chocolate, as anyone old enough to have experienced the 1970s will testify. Remember the much-maligned menu classic, Black Forest gateau?

They also are the traditional fruit in my go-to emergency dessert clafoutis, a quick-to-prepare batter with a layer of cherries that comes together to create a soothing, warming dessert perfect for almost every season.

Both sour and sweet cherries can be preserved using the following method and used as pie fillings among other things, including the filling of a cake – I'm thinking a big thick chocolate cake.

Makes approx. 1 litre (2 US pints)
—

500ml (1 US pint) water
80g (3oz) sugar
600g (1lb 5oz) cherries, pitted

1. Combine the water and sugar in a pan and heat over a medium heat until the sugar is completely dissolved.

2. Put the cherries into warm, sterilised jars and top up with syrup, leaving a 2.5cm (1 inch) airspace. Remove any air bubbles. Wipe the rim of the jars and put on the lids. Process in a boiling water bath for 25 minutes.

Store in a cool, dark place for up to a year. Once opened, refrigerate and consume within one month.

Blackcurrant coulis

Blackcurrants are quite common in the UK but not so common in the US, particularly in New York State, as until recently they were illegal! They were a vector for a disease – white pine blister rust – that killed a lot of pine trees, but now you can legally grow them again. They are gaining in popularity, although it still takes some looking to find them even in farmers' markets in the US. For this reason, when I see them at the market I grab them and try to find as many ways to save them as possible. Cassis sorbet is one of them, but this sauce is another way to eke out the bounty.

Makes approx. 500ml (1 US pint)
—

700g (1½lb) blackcurrants
100ml (about ½ cup) water
125g (4½oz) sugar

1. Put all of the ingredients in a heavy-bottomed pan and heat gently while stirring until the sugar has dissolved. Increase the heat and cover with a lid and continue cooking until almost all of the currants have popped, about 5–10 minutes.

2. Pour the syrupy currants into a fine-mesh sieve over a bowl and push everything through with a wooden spoon so all you are left with are seeds and some skin.

3. Fill some sterilised jars and seal. Process in a hot-water canner for 15 minutes. Allow to stand for 12 hours untouched. After the first hour, check the jars are correctly sealed.

This keeps unopened for three to four months in the refrigerator. Once opened, eat within seven to ten days.

Cranberry and orange relish

Perfect with turkey: think large scale for Christmas or Thanksgiving (a perfect example of preserving seasonal produce for use on a festive occasion later in the year), or smaller scale in a turkey or chicken sandwich, equally good. Tangy and tart, a good counterbalance.

Makes 0.5 litre (2 us pints)
—

500g (1lb 2oz) cranberries, rinsed
60ml (4 tbsp) maple syrup
Zest and juice of 2 oranges (about 200ml, ¾ cup)
¼ tsp ground cloves
50g (1¾oz) demerara sugar

1. Have warm sterilised jars and lids and a canning pot of boiling water ready.

2. Add all the ingredients to a medium-large pan and mix to combine everything. Heat gently until the sugar dissolves, then increase the heat a little to get it bubbling. Boil gently for a few minutes, until say two-thirds of the cranberries have popped but not all. You want some of them to remain whole to keep the texture chunkier.

3. Fill the jars, leaving a 12mm (½ inch) airspace and tap gently to remove any air bubbles from the jars. Wipe the jar rims, put the lids on and tighten to finger-tight. Process for 15 minutes and check for proper seal after 1 hour. Don't move the jars for 12 hours.

Keep in a cool, dark place and use within a year. Once opened, refrigerate and consume within three months.

Crushed tomatoes

We use so many tomatoes throughout the year, whether in salads and straight off the vine at the height of the summer, to make a myriad of dishes, pasta and pizza sauce, and in many braised dishes in the winter ... tomatoes are comforting and delicious all at once.

We await the arrival of the first tomatoes with excitement and then as the last ones disappear from our vines or the farmers' market, we lament the passing of summer. I try to preserve as many tomatoes as I can, knowing that it will never be enough to last me through the rest of the year without ever purchasing a tin of tomatoes from the supermarket.

This recipe is a way to preserve tomatoes with minimum fuss and allows the flexibility of use that a tin of tomatoes provides. I typically use a mix of plum and heritage tomatoes but you can stick to one type knowing that non-plum tomatoes will yield a lot more liquid.

Makes approx. 1 litre (2 US pints)
—

2¼kg (5lb) tomatoes
Citric acid as required

1. Fill a large pan with water and bring to the boil. Meanwhile score a cross in each tomato with a sharp knife. Fill a large bowl with cold water. When the water in the pan is boiling put a few tomatoes in the pan for 30–45 seconds and then remove and put immediately in the bowl of cold water. Repeat with the rest of the tomatoes. Drain the tomatoes and peel each one – the skin will have already started to peel from the cross – and remove the central core.

2. Over a large pan squeeze each tomato in your hand to break it into 3–5 pieces depending on how big the tomatoes are. You want the tomato to be broken up with all the juices and seeds also going into the pan.

3. Fill your canning pan with hot water and bring to the boil, and get your sterilised jars warmed and ready. I use a mixture of 750ml and 1-litre jars (1½ pint and quart jars) as quite often I find a smaller tin not quite enough when I am making something for my family of four with some leftovers remaining.

4. Heat the pan of tomatoes over a medium-high heat until boiling. Boil for 5 minutes.

5. With your warmed jars ready, add ¼ teaspoon per 500ml (1 US pint) citric acid to each jar. Add the tomatoes, leaving a 1.25cm (½ inch) airspace. Tap the bottom of the jars to remove any air bubbles. Wipe the rims, put on the lids and tighten. Process in your hot-water canner for 35 minutes for the 750ml jars and 40 minutes for the litre jars.

These will keep in a cool, dark spot for up to a year. Once opened, refrigerate and use within five days.

Salted nasturtium seeds

Recipes

Salt

The use of salt to preserve foods (pickling, fermentation and dry curing) was originally brought about through necessity. Without stores of meat, fish and vegetables to eat throughout the harsh winters in days gone by people would have starved. It is true also that while we may not need to rely on salt for food preservation in today's modern world, as humans we still need salt to survive.

Most harmful bacteria cannot survive in a salty environment, which makes salt-cured foods safe to eat even after being stored for prolonged periods of time. Preserving meat and fish with salt, known as 'curing', requires a certain level of skill – and it is certainly something you wouldn't wish to get wrong. Vegetables, though, are a lot easier to deal with – I would even go so far as to say that making the kraut (fermented cabbage) on page 105 is one of the easiest preserved foods you could make.

Brine crops up frequently in this chapter. It is a solution made up of salt and water, used for pickling and fermentation (as a general rule a brine should contain at least 5% salt). A brine can also be used to draw water out of vegetables as preparation prior to preserving through other methods, keeping them crisp and less likely to spoil over time.

Fruit and vegetables can also be preserved solely in salt – lemon and capers being prime examples – where the fruit is packed into jars inbetween layers of salt.

The recipes in this chapter are very low-tech – anyone can do this, anywhere. All you need is great produce, salt and a suitable vessel to make and store your preserved foods in.

Clockwise from top
Sauerkraut with caraway seeds, Ramp kimchi, Sauerkraut with mint, Carrot and ginger ferment, Red cabbage and apple kraut

Sauerkraut with caraway seeds

While I know this would be a complete no-no in today's world – where children under one should not eat salt (and for good reason, of course) – I was fed sauerkraut with knoedel (German dumplings) and gravy as one of my first proper meals.

My mother tells me stories of how her great-aunt used to make huge ceramic vats of kraut and stamp on the cabbage with her feet to create a brine. We still have her infamous sauerkraut vessel, in fact, although as I never make such vast quantities, her pot now houses flowers in our front garden.

This recipe is for a raw kraut. I use caraway seeds as that is the classic German way – it is about as simple a kraut recipe as it gets. Anybody can make this and I urge you to.

I eat raw kraut alongside other things, a bit like a side salad or spooned on top of dishes – perfect on goulash or winter stew, delicious in sandwiches (I especially like it with cream cheese and apple on sourdough bread, or in a sandwich with pastrami and mustard). Of course, it sits most perfectly alongside a grilled sausage.

Makes 750ml (1½ US pints)
—

1 medium white cabbage (approx. 1.2kg, 2½lb)
½ tsp caraway seeds
2½–3 tsp salt

1. Peel the outer leaves off the cabbage – I leave the core in but you can cut it out if you prefer. Slice the cabbage into thin strips (about 3mm thick) – I prefer to use a knife rather than a food processor, as I find the latter makes a softer-textured kraut and I like it crunchy. Place the shredded cabbage and caraway seeds in a bowl and sprinkle with salt as you go.

SALT

2. Now comes the fun bit: roll up your sleeves and scrunch the cabbage in your hands for about 10 minutes to draw out the moisture. It may not look like it, but after 10 minutes you should have created enough brine to completely cover the cabbage.

3. Pack the cabbage into a jar, a little at a time, pressing it down firmly with your hand or kitchen implement as you go. Once the cabbage is packed tightly with enough brine to completely cover it, fill a smaller (very clean) jar with water and place it on top of the kraut to weigh it down and prevent the cabbage from floating up to the surface. Cover with a clean tea towel and set aside in a cool place for between 5 days and 2 weeks.

4. Test your kraut as the days go by – at 5 days it will be a very young sauerkraut (I actually like it best at 7 days). After 2 weeks the fermented flavour will be quite strong. When the taste is right for you, remove the jar full of water, seal with a lid and store in the fridge ready to use.

A raw kraut will keep well in the fridge for up to six months – the flavour will intensify slightly as time goes by.

Alternative: Sauerkraut with mint
Follow the recipe above but instead of caraway seeds use 20 fresh mint leaves (shredded).

Red cabbage and apple kraut with juniper berries

Traditionally red cabbage is flavoured with juniper berries in Germany. On Sundays it is made with apples to go alongside roast pork. This recipe is essentially a fermented, raw version of red cabbage. This is particularly nice as an alternative vegetable accompaniment on Christmas Day, or with a cold turkey sandwich.

Makes 1.5 litres (3 US pints)

—

1 medium red cabbage (approx. 1.2kg, 2½lb)
2 eating apples (approx. 250g, 9oz), peeled and grated
12 juniper berries
5 tsp salt

1. Follow the same method as the sauerkraut with caraway seeds recipe. Simply replace the caraway seeds with juniper berries. Once you have sprinkled the cabbage and berries with salt, add the apple.

2. As before, test your kraut as the days go by. When the taste is right for you, remove the water-filled jar, seal the jar with the lid and store in the fridge until ready to use.

A raw kraut will keep well in the fridge for up to six months – the flavour will continue to intensify slightly as time goes by.

Carrot and ginger ferment

Sweet, hot and sour. This recipe combines sweetness from the carrots, heat from the ginger and sourness from the fermentation process. It makes the perfect condiment alongside rice dishes.

Makes 400ml (just under 1 US pint)
—

450g (1lb) carrots, grated
40g (1½oz) ginger, peeled and finely grated
2½ tsp salt

1. Place the carrots and ginger in a bowl, sprinkling in the salt as you go. Scrunch this mixture with your hands to draw out the moisture. After five minutes the carrots should be very moist with brine.

2. Pack the carrots into a jar, a little at a time, pressing them down firmly with your hand or kitchen implement as you go. Once the carrot is packed tightly with enough brine to completely cover it, fill a smaller (very clean) jar with water and place it on top of the carrot to weigh it down. Cover this with a clean tea towel and set aside in a cool place for anything between 5 days and 2 weeks.

3. Test your carrots as the days go by – at 5 days it will be a very young ferment but the sour flavour should be coming through. After 2 weeks the fermented flavour will be quite strong. The carrots will compress as the days go by, so you will end up with what looks like a smaller quantity. When the taste is right for you, remove the jar full of water, seal the kraut up and store in the fridge ready to use.

This should keep well in the fridge for up to six months – the flavour will intensify slightly as time goes by.

Vegetable soup mix

This salty mixture is my best friend in the kitchen. Think of it like a stock cube – great for an instant broth, fabulous in stews, soups and sauces. I grew up with my mother adding it to so many things, she grew up with her mother using it, whose mother also used it, and so it goes on for a few more generations back.

The oldest version I have is my great-grandmother's recipe; she used parsley roots, which give a wonderful earthy flavour. I realise that not everyone has a garden full of parsley – so if you are lucky enough to have the roots, make sure you use them; if not it's not the end of the world. I add a little fennel to my recipe these days as I like the warm aniseed flavour it gives.

Makes 1.5 litres (3 US pints)
—

300g (11oz) leeks, washed and trimmed
100g (3½oz) parsley
250g (9oz) carrots
250g (9oz) celeriac (with leaves)
100g (3½oz) fennel (optional – or use 100g of carrots
    or celeriac)
400g (14oz) salt

1. Put all of the vegetables into a food processor and blitz to a grainy paste.

2. Tip into a bowl and mix in the salt.

3. Pack tightly into sterilised jars and seal.

Store in a cool, dark place and it will keep well for up to one year.
Once opened, store in the fridge and it will keep for another six months.
The vegetable mix will discolour the longer it is kept but this has no impact on flavour and it is still perfectly fine to use.

Salted nasturtiums

Nasturtiums grow well and self-seed. If you have them in your garden, or know someone who does, this – along with the recipe for pickled nasturtium seeds on page 64 – is a fun recipe. This is my take on the intense salty capers imported from Italy and Spain. Lovely in salads, pasta dishes and on pizzas.

Makes 200ml (approx. ½ US pint)
—

50g (2oz) salt flakes, or sea salt is fine
50g (2oz) large chunky salt crystals
Some freshly picked nasturtium seeds (2 handfuls
is enough)

1. Pick the nasturtium seeds when still green, gathering enough to fill a small jar.

2. Place seeds in a bowl and toss in the salt flakes or sea salt, leave for 48 hours.

3. Strain and rinse off the salt and pat dry. Pop in a jar, mixing it with the large chunky salt crystals.

Store in a cool, dark place. It will be ready within one month and will keep for six. A small amount of liquid will collect at the bottom of the jar. This is excess liquid coming out of the seeds, and nothing to worry about. Rinse off before use to remove excess saltiness.

Ramp kimchi

Kimchi is made out of pungent, spicy, fermented raw vegetables. Originally from Korea, it is gaining global popularity these days. Use it as a condiment to go in sandwiches or to top rice dishes, soups and stews.

Makes 2 litres (4 us pints)
—

**50g (2oz) ramps (wild garlic), bulbs and leaves –
    or just leaves is fine**
250g (9oz) carrots, peeled
500g (1lb) red cabbage, thinly sliced
1 tsp chilli flakes
2½ tsp salt
3cm (1¼ inch) piece of ginger

1. Carefully clean and thinly slice the ramps. Place in a large bowl. Julienne (cut into fine matchsticks) the carrots by hand, or by using a mandolin or a food processor. Add the carrots and the cabbage to the bowl along with the rest of the ingredients. Scrunch it all together, squeezing hard. You want the vegetables to start giving up some of their liquids.

2. Keep scrunching for a few minutes until the juices start flowing; it takes a while to get them started, but once they do it gets easier. There needs to be enough liquid to cover the contents once they are packed into jars. I use two 1-litre (us quart) jars for this recipe.

3. When you think you have enough liquid, pack all the vegetables into the jars and use any extra liquid to top up to ensure contents are fully immersed. Set the jars somewhere out on the work surface where they can stand undisturbed for 3–5 days.

4. Fill a couple of very clean 500ml (1 US pint) jars with water and place them in the filled quart jars to weigh down the vegetables in the liquid. Cover them with a clean tea towel. Leave them, checking daily that there is enough liquid.

5. Start checking after 3 days – some people like kimchi a little less assertive than others. When they have reached the desired taste cover the jars with clean lids and place in the refrigerator.

This stores well for at least a month; the flavour will develop over time and may at some point get too sour for some tastes. Make sure you always use a super-clean utensil to take the kimchi out of the jar.

Preserved lemons

Preserved lemons are super-easy to make and cost quite a lot to buy, two good reasons to make them yourself. They are used a lot in Middle Eastern and North African cooking to add a citrusy burst of freshness to dishes. Make them when lemons are plentiful and good value. These take up more room at the beginning of the process so I generally make them in two or three jars and then transfer them once they squish down and as they release their juices in the salt.

Makes ... as many as you want!
—

4–6 lemons, washed, per 500ml (1 US pint) jar
1 tbsp coarse sea salt per lemon
1–2 dried red chillis per jar (optional)
4–5 peppercorns per jar (optional)
1–2 bay leaves per jar (optional)

1. Take a couple of sterilised jars of whatever size you would like to use, but 500ml (1 US pint) is probably the easiest as you need a wide mouth to get the lemons in easily.

2. Cut the lemons in a cross shape from the bottom end (i.e. the end that was *not* attached to the tree). Cut the cross deep, almost to the stalk end, but keep the stalk end connected so the lemons remain attached.

3. Stuff about 1 tbsp of coarse salt into the cross of each lemon and put the lemons in the jar. Squish them in tightly. Add any of the spices you choose now.

4. Cover and put in a cool, dark place for about 5–7 days. Every day shake the jar and if necessary push the lemons down with the handle of a wooden spoon. Gradually over the course of a few days liquid will be released from the lemons. The liquid should cover the lemons entirely.

5. At the end of that time they should be refrigerated. If the lemons take up a lot less space in the jar you could transfer them to a smaller sterilised jar or amalgamate several jars if you like, making sure they remain covered in the juice/brine.

The lemons will last for a year if you make sure you use a very clean spoon whenever you remove any from the jar. To use, remove and discard the flesh of the lemons and use the rind.

SALT

5
Oil

Recipes

Oil

Oil

**As stated in the introduction to this book, the four
elements that cause decay in food are bacteria, mould,
yeast and enzymes. They thrive in air, so the easiest
way to prevent these intruders from spoiling our food
is through blocking their air supply.**

Oil does not just serve as the barrier between the food
and the surrounding air, it also plays an important part
in flavouring whatever it is we are preserving, which is
why it's always important to choose the right kind of oil
from the start.

Extra-virgin olive oil is strong and fruity; it comes from
the first cold-pressing of the whole olives, hence its name.
While absolutely delicious, it can be too strong a flavour
for preserving, which is why it is mainly used mixed with
other, less flavour-intrusive, oils for this purpose.

Olive oil (or light olive oil) is of lower quality than
extra-virgin but for this reason it is also less fruity in
flavour, which means it works very well as an oil for
preserves.

Sunflower oil is light in colour and flavour, in fact it is
almost flavourless, which makes it the perfect oil to use
when preserving.

There are, of course, many other types of oil around, so feel free to experiment. Rapeseed oil (canola oil is a US alternative) has a deep nutty flavour. Almond oil, while not really suitable for cooking, as it doesn't do well when heated to high temperatures, has a delicate flavour and can be used in preserves.

The four key things to remember when preserving under oil are:

— **All produce must be clean**

— **All produce must be dry**

— **All produce must be completely covered by the oil**

— **Make sure there are no air bubbles trapped in the oil** – to do this tap the jar gently on the work surface to dispel them before sealing

Fennel confit

Fennel seems to be one of those vegetables you either love or hate. I love its warm, aniseed flavour. If, like me, you are a fennel lover, then this recipe is for you. It is perfect alongside white fish, with risotto, added to salads or simply eaten on its own with a slice of bread. If you are left with a jar of oil at the end don't waste it, use it to fry fish, drizzle over salads or dunk bread in.

Makes approx. 1.25 litres (2½ us pints)

650g (1lb 7oz) fennel with fronds (approx. 2 large bulbs)
½ tsp fennel seeds
1 tsp salt
3 strips lemon zest
400ml (1¾ cups) extra-virgin olive oil
300ml (1¼ cups) rapeseed oil

1. Heat the oven to 150°c / 300°f / Gas mark 2.

2. Place the fennel bulbs base-up on a chopping board and slice downwards, cutting ½cm (¼ inch) thick pieces – you want the fennel to hold together as a whole slice – so you end up with beautiful cross-sections of fennel.

3. Lay the fennel slices into the bottom of a large-lidded pan – I like to use a cast-iron pan but a normal saucepan also works. Sprinkle over the fennel seeds, salt and lemon zest.

4. Pour over the olive oil and top off with the rapeseed oil, making sure the oil covers the fennel completely. Use a wooden spoon to push it down if it isn't completely covered.

5. Pop the lid on the pan and place in the oven for 1 hour, by which time the fennel will be tender and slightly opaque.

6. Let the fennel cool down a little, then transfer into sterilised jars – I use tongs for this as it's quite tricky fitting the fennel in. Pour the oil over the top, ensuring that it completely covers the fennel. Seal and store in the fridge.

This keeps well for up to four weeks but it is important to only use scrupulously clean tongs/forks when taking the fennel out of the jar. The salt will draw out a little water from the fennel, creating a layer of brine at the bottom of the jars (this is nothing to worry about). The oil will congeal slightly in the fridge, so if using the fennel in a salad it is a good idea to take it out of the fridge for ten minutes before use to allow it to 'melt' back to room temperature.

Artichokes in oil

Artichokes in oil

If you are lucky enough to grow or have access to young artichokes this recipe is a stunner, and a delicious preserve to have squirrelled away in your fridge for a rainy day. Artichokes are delicious on an antipasti platter – as you would use sun-dried tomatoes – or on homemade pizzas or warmed over pasta with lots of Parmesan.

Makes 600ml (1¼ US pints)
—

8 small young artichoke heads
Small bunch of parsley, chopped roughly
2 garlic cloves, chopped roughly
300ml (1¼ cups) extra-virgin olive oil to cover
Salt and pepper

1. Cut the artichoke heads in half, or quarters, so they are all roughly the same size, cut off and discard the tough stems or leaves. Put the artichokes into a pan so that they all fit, add parsley and garlic. Cover with olive oil and slowly warm through, cooking for 30 minutes until tender. Stir in a pinch of salt and pepper.

2. Allow to cool.

3. Put the artichokes into the sterilised jar, cover with the cooking oil and allow to settle. Cover the jar with a lid and gently bang the jar to allow any air bubbles to escape the oil.

Keeps in the fridge for up to six weeks. The oil may solidify but will soften as it comes to room temperature. After using the artichokes, the leftover oil is beautiful to cook with, and can be kept in the fridge until you are ready to use it.

Garden vegetables under oil

This recipe stems from the wonderful Italian pickle 'La Giardiniera', basically a mixture of pickled garden vegetables. These are the most versatile of pickles and pair well with any cheese, but are especially good with cold meats.

There are many ways to make La Giardiniera. Some recipes preserve the vegetables in a vinegar brine with only a splash of oil added at the end, others use equal measures of oil to vinegar. This recipe 'pickles' the vegetables in a vinegar brine, which keeps them crisp for longer, then preserves them under oil.

Any firm vegetables may be used here but the following are the most common – celery, bell peppers, carrots, cauliflower, fennel, green beans, onions, shallots, chillis, garlic and aubergine (eggplant in US).

My rule is this: for every 1.5kg (3½lb) of vegetables you need 2 litres (4¼ US pints) of brine. It doesn't really matter what combination of vegetables you use but the quantities stated in this recipe give a good overall balance.

Makes approx. 1.4 litres (2½ US pints)
—

125g (4½oz) green beans, trimmed
125g (4½oz) small shallots, peeled
100g (3½oz) fennel (approx. 1 small bulb) cut into
**   10 wedges (still attached at the base)**
150g (5oz) cauliflower (approx. half a cauliflower),
**   cut into bite-sized florets**
150g (5oz) carrots (if the carrots are small enough
**   they may be left whole, otherwise quarter them**
**   lengthways or slice into 1cm / ½ inch chunks)**
100g (3½oz) red bell pepper (approx. 1 small pepper),
**   sliced into 1cm / ½ inch-thick strips**
100g (3½oz) salt
500ml (1 US pint) white wine vinegar

500ml (1 US pint) water
½ tsp black peppercorns
½ tsp pink peppercorns
225ml (1 cup) rapeseed oil (canola in the us)
300ml (1¼ cup) olive oil (not extra virgin)

1. Place all the prepared vegetables into a large bowl. Pour the salt over the top, followed by the vinegar and water. It is important that the vegetables are completely covered by liquid, so weigh the vegetables down with a sterilised plate to completely immerse them (the cauliflower has a habit of floating to the surface). Cover the bowl with a clean tea towel and leave to stand overnight in a cool place.

2. The following day, drain the liquid off and if you don't plan to reuse in any other recipe, simply dispose of it. Spread the drained vegetables onto a clean tea towel and allow them to 'air dry' for 2 hours.

3. Pack the vegetables tightly into sterilised jars along with the peppercorns. Pour over the rapeseed (canola) oil followed by the olive oil. The vegetables should be completely immersed, if they aren't just top up with olive oil until covered. Tap the jars gently on the work surface to dispel any air bubbles, seal and leave in a cool, dark place for 2 weeks before eating.

Keeps well stored in a cool, dark place for up to a year. Once opened, no need to refrigerate, but consume within a month. (If refrigerated, once opened, they will keep for up to three months).

Slow-roast tomatoes in oil

These slow-roasted tomatoes burst with flavour. Cooking the tomatoes slowly enhances the sunshine taste. They are gorgeous as antipasti, in sandwiches, salads, and warmed over pasta. Also lovely popped into a large dish with fish and fennel confit, over a bed of thinly sliced new potatoes and roasted for a quick and simple supper.

Makes 400ml (just under 1 US pint)
—

400g (14oz) cherry tomatoes, cut in half
2 tbsp extra-virgin olive oil plus roughly 300ml (1¼ cups)
     to cover
2 sprigs fresh thyme
Salt and pepper

1. Preheat the oven to 150°C / 300°F / Gas mark 2.

2. Place the tomatoes on an oiled baking tray, sprinkle with thyme leaves, salt and pepper and a drizzle more oil. Place the tray into the oven for 1 hour. The tomatoes will be soft and sweet. Allow to cool thoroughly.

3. Pop the tomatoes into a sterilised jar, cover with oil, allow to settle. Cover the jar with a lid and gently tap the jar to allow any air bubbles to escape the oil.

This will keep refrigerated for up to two weeks. The oil may solidify but will soften as it comes to room temperature. After using the tomatoes the leftover oil is beautiful to cook with; I like to roast vegetables in it.

Baked sewin with slow-roast
tomatoes and fennel confit

Celeriac under oil

Celeriac is a delicious but under-used vegetable. Its subtle flavour is enhanced by roasting. This is lovely as an antipasti or with pasta and lots of chilli and Parmesan.

Makes 400ml (just under 1 US pint)
—

1 large whole celeriac, or 2 smaller ones, peeled, sliced
    1cm (½inch) thick and cut into sizes to fit into jars
200ml (¾ cup) extra-virgin olive oil
Salt and pepper
2–4 small cloves garlic, peeled

1. Preheat the oven to 170°C / 325°F / Gas mark 3.

2. Oil a large baking sheet and spread the celeriac out, drizzle oil over it, and salt and pepper. Roast for 18 minutes until tender, turning once. Allow to cool completely.

3. Place celeriac into jars, adding 2 garlic cloves to each jar, and top up with olive oil until covered. Tap gently to remove any hidden air bubbles.

Keeps in a cool, dark place for four months. Once opened, eat within two weeks.

Garlic confit

Garlic confit is one of those things that is great to have in your pantry as it's so versatile. It can be used in anything that you would use garlic in but will give a more subtle, gentle flavour than plain raw garlic.

Makes approx. 500ml (1 us pint)
—

2 heads garlic, broken up into cloves
Olive oil as required

1. Peel the garlic cloves and put in a small saucepan. Cover with olive oil. Heat the pan slowly and allow to barely simmer for about 45–60 minutes. You want the garlic cloves to become very soft but still whole and not falling apart.

2. Fill a sterilised jar with the cloves and top off with the remaining oil. All the cloves should be submerged in the oil.

Keep refrigerated and use within two weeks.

Oil

Strawberry cordial

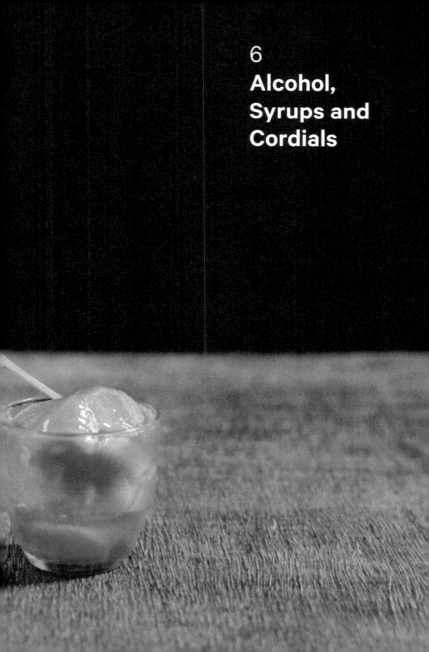

6
**Alcohol,
Syrups and
Cordials**

Recipes

Alcohol, Syrups and Cordials

This chapter is mostly about preserving fruit and its flavours in alcohol. There is hardly anything to it really. At the most basic level it is a simple mixture of fruit / sugar / alcohol – you could argue that it's hard to mess up. There is just one hard fact: Spirits used to preserve fruit must be at least 40 per cent alcohol by volume (UK), equivalent to 80 per cent proof (US).

Gin, vodka, brandy, whisky and rum are all fitting spirits to use. There are no real rules – experiment with what flavours work best with each other. Use honey instead of sugar, add spices for a deeper flavour and fresh herbs for zing. Play around, be creative.

Unlike a jam, which is ready in a matter of hours from start to finish, the only drawback of using alcohol to preserve is that it takes time. A fruit liqueur or schnapps can take a few months to mature. On the plus side, it is not a labour-intensive process – the fruit and alcohol need time to mingle with each other, during which time you do nothing to it. It couldn't be simpler and is well worth the wait.

It is good practice to use sterilised bottles and jars when preserving with alcohol. Make sure seals to bottles and jars are intact, as otherwise the alcohol will evaporate.

Strawberry and mint shrub

A shrub is an old-fashioned thirst quencher that harks back to ancient times. It is basically a syrup of fruit and vinegar, which is diluted with chilled water to produce a most delicious drink.

The beauty of the shrub is that it doesn't rely on the produce used being the best quality. Making a shrub is a great way to use up very ripe (on the turn) fruit – perfect for garden gluts.

The shrub fell out of fashion with the rise of fizzy soft drinks but is making a comeback. While the shrub itself is non-alcoholic, it makes a wonderful fruity addition to cocktails.

Makes approx. 450ml (just under 1 US pint)
—

250g (9oz) strawberries, hulled and quartered
12 mint leaves
250g (9oz) sugar
200ml (¾ cup) white wine vinegar

1. Place the strawberries, mint and sugar in a bowl, stir, cover and set aside on the work surface for 8 hours or overnight. After this time the sugar should have dissolved to form a syrup. If the sugar hasn't quite dissolved, stir the mixture until the grains have disappeared.

2. Place the fruit mixture into a sieve over a bowl to separate the syrup from the pulp and mint leaves. You can help this along by using the back of a spoon to push the pulp against the sieve and release the syrup. This should yield around 250ml (1½ US pint) of syrup.

3. Pour the syrup and the vinegar into a sterilised jar, seal and shake to mix.

Store the shrub in the fridge. It will keep for up to six months.

Strawberry gin fizz

A lovely fresh aperitif, perfect for the summer months.

Makes 300ml (1¼ cups), enough for 2 glasses
—

50ml (4 tbsp) gin
50ml (4 tbsp) strawberry and mint shrub (see previous recipe)
2 mint leaves
2 cucumber slices
250ml (1 cup) soda water
Ice as required

1. Half-fill two old-fashioned juice glasses with ice. Pour half the gin and half the shrub into each glass, add the mint leaves and cucumber slices, top with soda water and stir.

Apple and thyme shrub

This shrub has an earthy note because of the thyme and is a really good non-alcoholic accompaniment to a meal. You can use any eating apples for this, but the flavour will vary greatly. I use a favourite variety of mine, Cox's Orange Pippin, which make a vibrant, fruity shrub. Ruby McIntosh apples work well and make a sweeter drink. Something like a Granny Smith makes a tart shrub, which I am less keen on – but tastes vary, so suit yourself and use your favourite variety of apple.

Makes approx. 450ml (just under 1 US pint)
—

250g (9oz) eating apples, grated (not peeled)
250g (9oz) demerara sugar
5 sprigs of thyme
**250ml (½ US pint) apple cider vinegar (I use the
    unfiltered variety as I find the flavour more
    robust, but it doesn't really matter)**

1. Place the apple, sugar and thyme into a clean bowl, stir, cover with a tea towel and set aside on the work surface for 8 hours or overnight. After this time the sugar should have dissolved to form a syrup. If the sugar hasn't quite dissolved, stir the mixture around until the grains have disappeared.

2. Place the fruit mixture into a sieve over a bowl to catch the liquid. This should yield about 250ml (½ US pint) of syrup.

3. Pour the syrup and the vinegar into a sterilised jar, seal and shake to mix.

Store the shrub in the fridge. It will keep for up to six months.

Strawberry gin

This is a bit of fun for a summer's day, a party or a cocktail. Lovely sipped with ice and a squeeze of lime as an aperitif to brighten up your day.

Makes 350ml (¾ us pint)
—

300g (11oz) strawberries, chopped into large pieces, stems and bruised bits removed
300ml (1¼ cups) gin
75g (2½oz) granulated sugar

1. Pop the fruit and gin into a jar, ensuring the fruit is completely covered, and store in a cool, dark place overnight.

2. Strain the mixture through a muslin, reserving the liquid. Use a funnel to put the juice and sugar into a bottle, shaking every day until the sugar is dissolved. Your gin is ready to enjoy.

Store in a cool, dark place and drink within the year.

Cassis

A beautiful-looking vivid liquor evocative of summer.
Tasty drizzled over ice cream, in sorbets or best of all pour
a little into white wine for a 'Kir' or in Cava, Prosecco or
Champagne for a 'Kir Royale' – delicious.

Makes roughly 1 litre (2 US pints)
—

**500g (1lb 2oz) blackcurrants, freshly picked and
    checked through**
500ml (1 US pint) brandy or vodka
200g (7oz) granulated sugar

1. Place the blackcurrants into the jar and cover with the
   brandy (or vodka if you wish). Seal and leave in a cool,
   dark place for at least 6 weeks.

2. Strain the blackcurrants through a muslin and keep the
   liquor. Mix the blackcurrant liquor with the sugar in the
   bottle you will finally store it in.

3. Shake the mixture twice a day until the sugar is fully
   dissolved. Sugar here is a matter of taste – you might
   want to use a bit more or less, so try once it's made.

This will keep for up to one year in a cool, dark cupboard.

Rhubarb gin

This is a simple and also quite sophisticated way of capturing the fresh tang of rhubarb in a bottle. It's lovely to sip on its own, for a G&T with a difference, or as an addition to a cocktail for a bit of fun.

Makes 500ml (1 US pint)

—

**250g (9oz) rhubarb (the pinker the better) chopped
into 1.5cm (¾ inch) pieces**
400ml (1¾ cups) gin
120g (4¼oz) granulated sugar

1. Put the fruit in the jar, and completely cover with gin. Store in a cool, dark place for 1 week.

2. Strain the mixture through a muslin, reserving the liquid. Pour it, with the sugar, back into the bottle. A funnel might be useful. Shake the bottle every day until the sugar is dissolved.

3. Your gin is ready to enjoy – just add ice and tonic!

Store in a cool, dark place and drink within the year.

Blueberry, mint and lime cordial

Fruity and zesty, this cordial packs a real punch.

Makes approx. 1 litre (2 US pints)
—

500ml (1 US pint) lime juice (approx. 16 limes)
30 mint leaves
500g (1lb) blueberries
650g (1lb 7oz) sugar
500ml (1 US pint) water

1. Put all the ingredients into a saucepan and bring to the boil, stirring occasionally to dissolve the sugar. Boil for 10 minutes (no more, otherwise you will be making a jelly).

2. Pour the syrup through a sieve to separate the blueberries and mint leaves.

3. Bottle in sterilised jars while still hot. Seal and allow to cool before storing in the fridge.

This will keep for a month.

Note:
Don't throw away the blueberries, mix them with some apples and use them in a pie.

Strawberry cordial

A lovely quick and simple way of using up overripe and damaged fruit when you have plenty. There is nothing like a fresh, cool glass of fruity cordial on a hot summer's day. This cordial is fabulous as it is, but great poured over yogurt or ice cream, and superb in cocktails. You can also use up rhubarb, plums and other berries in the same way. This is a great treat for the kids when diluted with water – and with only two ingredients is far better than any squash full of unnecessary preservatives.

Makes 500ml (1 US pint)

—

400g (14oz) strawberries, hulled and halved if large
200g (7oz) sugar

1. Put the fruit and sugar into a pan with a couple of tablespoons of water, bring slowly to the boil and cook until the fruit is tender.

2. Strain the fruit through a muslin bag over a jug or bowl, catching all the syrup. Leave for 4 hours or overnight.

3. Bottle and store in the fridge.

This will keep for up to one month – if it lasts that long!

Elderberry syrup

Packed full of vitamin C, this syrup is brilliant for the winter months to help ward off colds. I especially enjoy it as a hot drink but it is also great cold or added to cocktails. Mixed with a little red wine vinegar and oil it makes a fruity salad dressing.

Makes approx. 500ml (1 us pint)
—

500g (1lb 2oz) elderberries
300ml (1¼ cups) water
300g (11oz) sugar
60ml (4 tbsp) lemon juice (approx. juice of 1 lemon)

1. Put the elderberries, water and sugar into a pan and bring to a boil, stirring to dissolve the sugar. Once boiling, turn the heat down and simmer for 25 minutes until all the berries have popped open and the liquid has reduced down to a syrup. Stir in the lemon juice.

2. Remove from the heat and strain through a muslin suspended over a jug. Pour into sterilised bottles and store in the fridge.

This will keep refrigerated for up to six months.

Note:
You can add spices to this recipe, for more of a 'mulled wine' flavour. Add a small cinnamon stick and 8 cloves to the pan at the start of cooking.

ALCOHOL, SYRUPS AND CORDIALS

Vanilla extract

This is hardly a recipe but I wanted to include it here as it really is so useful and saves buying the very expensive shop-bought stuff. Any strong alcohol can be used but I like the flavour of rum. However, vodka is the most neutral choice and you can argue it is the one that allows the vanilla to stand out the most.

Makes 100ml (about ½ cup)
—

**100ml (about ½ cup) golden or dark rum
    (or vodka, whisky, brandy)
2 vanilla pods, split lengthways**

1. Put the rum and vanilla pods into a sterilised jar, seal and leave to sit and infuse in a cool, dark place.

2. After 6 weeks the vanilla should have strongly infused the rum. There is no need to take the pods out when you use the extract – leaving them in will intensify the flavour. As the extract goes down just top it up with more rum.

Store in a cool, dark place and it will keep indefinitely.

Lemon balm liqueur

Lemon balm has a calming effect and has been used for centuries to ease digestion and aid sleep, which makes this liqueur the perfect drink after dinner and before bed. If you don't have your own supply of homegrown lemon balm, you can usually find it in the fresh herb section of specialised grocers.

Makes approx. 600ml (1¼ US pints)
—

30 lemon balm leaves
Zest of 2 unwaxed lemons
150g (5oz) sugar
500ml (1 US pint) vodka

1. Pop the lemon balm leaves, lemon zest and sugar into a large jar, pour over the vodka, seal and shake.

2. Store upright in a dark place for 4 weeks. Give the jar a shake every few days to help the sugar dissolve and stop it settling at the bottom of the jar.

3. After 4 weeks the liqueur should be full of flavour. Strain it through a sieve to remove the leaves and zest, then bottle.

Store sealed tightly in a cool, dark place and this will keep well for up to two years.

Note:
This same recipe can be made with any number of herbs in place of the lemon balm – try mint, basil or thyme.

Blackberry schnapps

This schnapps is based on the old-fashioned German drink but made using a less laborious process. No distilling involved here, you just add the fruit to alcohol.

Traditionally these drinks are not sweetened – any sweetness comes from the fruit alone. Personally I don't add any, but I have included honey in the recipe here for those with a sweeter palate.

Makes approx. 500ml (1 US pint)

—

200g (7oz) blackberries
500ml (1 US pint) vodka
Runny honey (optional – use 2 tbsp at a time)

1. Place the blackberries and vodka into a large sterilised jar, seal and shake. Allow to steep for 12 weeks in a cool, dark place, shaking the jar every 2 weeks.

2. Strain the vodka through a sieve – at this stage I just bottle the schnapps, but now is the perfect time to sweeten it.

3. Heat 2 tablespoons of honey in a small saucepan until it becomes more fluid. Add it to the bottle, seal and shake. Taste the schnapps after a week and repeat the sweetening process until you've found the perfect balance.

Store the schnapps upright in a cool, dark place and it will keep well for up to one year. The flavour on bottling will be fresh and fruity, but with time it becomes more intense.

Spiced orange rum

A drink for dusk – served over ice or as a hot toddy. I like mine on the sweeter side but you can adjust sugar quantities to suit taste.

Makes approx. 1 litre (2 US pints)
—

225ml (1 cup) freshly squeezed orange juice (juice of roughly 4 oranges)
150g (5oz) demerara sugar
750ml (1½ US pints) golden rum
4 strips of orange zest
1 vanilla pod, split lengthways
1 small cinnamon stick
6 cloves

1. Mix the orange juice and sugar together in a bowl, cover and set aside in the fridge overnight. After about 8 hours the sugar should have dissolved – if it hasn't, stir for a few minutes.

2. Put all the ingredients including the orange syrup into a large sterilised jar, seal and give it a little shake. Store upright in a cool, dark place for 3 weeks, by which time the rum should be sufficiently infused with the spices.

3. After 3 weeks, line a sieve with a muslin and pour the rum through to separate the spices and orange pulp. Fill suitable sterile bottles with the rum.

Store in a cool, dark place. Keeps for up to a year.

Plum liqueur

This is the German equivalent to our great British sloe gin / vodka. It is so versatile – perfect on its own, over ice, in cocktails, added to desserts and cakes or poured over ice cream.

Makes around 1.25 litres (2½ US pints)
—

750g (1lb 10oz) plums
500g (1lb 2oz) sugar
1 litre (2 US pints) vodka
1 small cinnamon stick

1. Slit the plums in half, pop out the stones and quarter. Place them into a large sterilised jar, tip over the sugar, pour over the vodka, add the cinnamon stick and seal the jar.

2. Give it a little shake to disperse the sugar and place in a cool, dark place for 6 weeks, tipping it up every 5 days and then placing it upright on its base again (this helps the sugar to dissolve and unsettle from the bottom).

3. After 6 weeks you should have a bright-red liqueur – at this point you can pass the liqueur through a sieve to remove the plums and cinnamon stick and re-bottle into sterilised vessels. But I like to keep the plums in and eat them as the liquid goes down (which it does rather rapidly in our house).

Store in a cool, dark place and it will keep for two years without the plums and for up to six months with the plums in.

Heisse Witwe

My very favourite way to drink the plum liqueur from the
previous recipe is as a hot drink called a Heisse Witwe
(Hot Widow). It is drunk in abundance on the snowy slopes
of Germany and Austria during the winter months. I love
the contrast of hot liqueur and cold cream.

Makes 200ml (about 1 us cup)

—

100ml (about ½ cup) double cream (heavy cream in the us)
200ml (about 1 cup) plum liqueur (from previous recipe)
¼ tsp ground cinnamon

1. Whip the cream till soft peaks form.

2. Heat the plum liqueur in a small saucepan and once hot
   pour into 4 large shot glasses, top with whipped cream
   and a pinch of cinnamon. Enjoy!

Plum liqueur

Prunes in brandy

These are utterly decadent and a real treat to have squirrelled away in your cupboard to nibble on after a cold winter's walk or as an after-dinner treat. They are very alcoholic, so not for children. Great served in a shot glass or over ice cream. You can play with the amount of sugar, adding more if you would like it sweeter.

Makes 1.5 litres (3 US pints)

—

200g (7oz) sugar
250ml (½ US pint) water
Lemon peel strips (from 1 lemon)
1 vanilla pod
500g (1lb 2oz) dried prunes
500ml (1 US pint) brandy

1. In a small pan mix the sugar and water and bring to the boil. Add strips of lemon peel, slice the vanilla pod in half and scrape out seeds, drop the pod into the pan. Boil for a couple of minutes and then pour the liquid over the prunes and leave to soak overnight.

2. Take the prunes out of the liquid and place in jars, mix the remaining liquid with the brandy and strain over the prunes.

3. Store in a cool, dark place, and they will be ready in 1 month.

Eat within six months.

Elderflower cordial

There are some things we make that mark a turning point in the year. Each new thing that appears in the hedgerow or at the farmers' market signals a change in season. Elderflower is one of my favourite things as it appears early in the season and is so fragrant in a totally floral way, whereas the winter is all about earthiness.

This cordial is both fruity and citrusy, and makes a truly refreshing drink whether you mix it with flat water, sparkling water or go all out and dilute it with Prosecco, Cava or Champagne. It is the taste of early summer.

Makes approx. 1 litre (2 US pints)
—

3 lemons
2 limes
900g (2lb) sugar
900ml (just under 2 US pints) water
Approx. 15 medium elderflower heads
1 tsp citric acid

1. Slice the lemons and limes thinly and set to one side.

2. Heat the sugar and water together in a large heavy-based pan over a medium heat, stirring occasionally until all the sugar is dissolved. Bring to a boil and then remove from the heat.

3. Add the citrus, flowers and citric acid, and stir well. Leave to cool and then allow to steep for 24–36 hours.

4. When steeped, drain through muslin or a fine sieve and pour into sterilised bottles or jars and seal. Keep in the refrigerator.

5. To serve add 1 part cordial to 5 parts water or fizz.

Fruit leathers and strawberry cordial

Recipes

Sugar-free

Today we are made increasingly aware of the negative effects that refined sugar has on us. A high intake of sugar causes our blood-sugar levels to spike, sending our pancreas into insulin production overdrive. Just recently there has been a surge of interest in unrefined sugars (honey, maple syrup, coconut sugar to name but a few) and, as a result, a 'healthier' wave of cooking and eating is emerging.

Fruit has its own natural sugar – fructose, which is very sweet. This sugar is absorbed more slowly into the body and doesn't shock the system in the same way sucrose (refined sugar) does. This chapter focuses on using fruit's own sugar as the 'sweetener' and 'preserver', without relying on any added extras.

High levels of sugar make an undesirable environment for enzymes and bacteria to thrive, thus making sugar an essential ingredient in preserving. In order to achieve these high sugar levels without adding extra sugar, fruit needs to be cooked down at a very slow rate over a long period of time. The following recipes take time and cannot be rushed, so patience, or a rainy Sunday afternoon, is required.

Powidl

Powidl (pronounced 'povidel') is a preserve traditionally made out of zwetschgen with no additional sweetners. Zwetschgen are plums grown in Bohemia and central Europe – the closest thing in the UK are damsons and elsewhere dark Italian plums.

My Bavarian great-grandmother used to make powidl in late September when the fruit was very ripe. Some say the best jam comes from those plums which have been kissed by the first frost – when their skins will break open easily – but as long as the fruit is fully ripe this is not necessary. If using damsons they must be extremely ripe and sweet; unripe damsons will result in a bitter spread.

Essentially this is a fruit butter, gently spiced and of melting consistency. It is perfect spread on toast, used in baked goods or added to sauces (like one might add redcurrant jelly) and is an excellent substitute in Chinese cooking for plum sauce.

Makes roughly 1.5 litres (3 us pints)
—

30ml (2 tbsp) water
2.5kg (5½ lb) zwetschgen, damsons or Italian plums
1 cinnamon stick (optional)
12 cloves (optional)

The method for this varies depending on the fruit used. For zwetschgen and Italian plums slit the fruit lengthways and pop the stone out. For damsons use the whole fruit as it is almost an impossible task trying to remove the stones.

1. Put the water into the bottom of the pan, add the fruit and spices, cover and bring to a simmer – this should take about half an hour – stirring occasionally to ensure the fruit does not stick. Once simmering, remove the

lid and turn the heat down low. Continue to simmer for about 3–3½ hours without the lid, stirring every 10 minutes to avoid sticking.

2. As the fruit simmers it will mush down into a pulp and become thicker. Towards the end of the 3 hours it is important to keep a watchful eye on the pan as this is when there is a risk of burning the fruit – at this stage I normally stand by the stove stirring constantly.

3. The powidl is ready when it coats a spoon like a thick sauce or custard. The skin of the fruit should have completely melted into the pulp and it should be deep burgundy-brown in colour (when cold it should be the consistency of butter at room temperature). You will need to pass the powidl through a sieve at this stage to remove the spices and, if using damsons, also the stones.

4. Pour the hot powidl into sterilised jars and seal.

Store in a cool, dark place. This will keep for up to a year – it may change in colour slightly the older it gets (from burgundy to brown). Once opened, store in the fridge and consume within four weeks.

Pear butter

This recipe uses a lot of pears for the amount of spread it produces. I normally use windfalls from the local common, which no one else seems to want or pick up. Although the yield isn't of great quantity, this is so very worth doing, especially when the fruit is picked for free.

It's quite hard to believe there is no sugar in this as it is deliciously sweet. Reminiscent of the classic British sweet-shop favourite, the pear drop, it is good eaten in all the usual ways – on hot buttered toast, with porridge, on rice pudding, dolloped on pancakes or pikelets and smothered on scones with cream.

Makes approx. 1 litre (2 US pints)
—

4kg (8¾lb) perfectly ripe pears, peeled and roughly diced
120ml (½ cup) lemon juice (approx. juice of 2 large lemons)
24 juniper berries

Any one of the following may be used as spice options in place of the juniper berries: 1 small cinnamon stick; 1 vanilla pod split lengthways; 20 whole cloves; 24 allspice berries.

1. Place the pears and lemon juice with the desired spice into a saucepan and bring to the boil with a lid on (this should only take about 5 minutes). Turn the heat down low and simmer the pears with the lid off for 2½–3 hours, stirring every 10 minutes to avoid sticking.

2. As the fruit simmers it will mush down into a pulp, reduce and become thicker. In the last half-hour it is important to keep a watchful eye on the pan as this is when there is a risk of burning the fruit – at this stage I normally stand by the stove stirring constantly.

3. You will notice the pears turn a lovely mellow pink colour in the last 30 minutes.

4. The butter is ready when it has the consistency of thick custard. Take the spices out and pass the spread through a sieve to squash out any lumps.

5. Pour the hot spread into hot sterilised jars and seal immediately.

Stored in a cool, dark place, this keeps well for six months. Once opened, store in the fridge and eat within three weeks.

Alternative: Pear and port sauce
For a unique sauce to be eaten alongside game or red meats, use the recipe above with the addition of port and extra lemon juice. Once the spread is cooked, add 100ml (about ½ cup) of port and 60ml (4 tbsp) of lemon juice, heat through, then pour into sterilised jars and store as above.

Apricot and vanilla spread

As this recipe is sugarless, it really must only be made with the most ripe, sweet apricots. The quantity for this recipe can be easily halved – the method is exactly the same.

Makes approx. 1.5 litres (3 US pints)
—

2kg (4½lb) apricots – remove stones and slice lengthways into quarters
200ml (¾ cup) water
60ml (4 tbsp) lemon juice (approx. juice of 1 large lemon)
1 vanilla pod, split lengthways

1. Place apricots in a saucepan with the water, lemon juice and vanilla pod. Bring to the boil with the lid on (this should take about 5 minutes).

2. Turn the heat down low and simmer the apricots with the lid off for 3 hours. It will mush down to a pulp and become thicker. Stir every 15 minutes to avoid sticking. Towards the end of the 3 hours stir continuously as there is a risk of burning the fruit on the bottom.

3. The spread is ready when it coats a spoon like a thick sauce or custard. The skin of the fruit should have completely dissolved into the pulp.

4. Take the vanilla pod out and, if so desired, pass the spread through a sieve to create a very smooth consistency (I tend not to bother for this particular spread).

5. Pour the spread into hot sterilised jars and seal immediately.

Stored in a cool, dark place, this keeps well for up to six months.
Once opened, store in the fridge and eat within four weeks.

Fruit leathers

A great healthy and simple snack for packed lunches and picnics, with nothing in it but fruit. The shop-bought versions just don't live up to it. Use any fruit in season.

Makes 8–10 snails (yes, snails!)
—

400g (14oz) strawberries (or plums, or rhubarb), hulls removed, and chopped
200g (7oz) apples, peeled, cored and chopped

1. Preheat oven to its lowest setting.

2. Place the chopped fruit in a pan with a lid and cook until soft, approx. 10 minutes. When cool, blend to a paste and sieve. Pour onto a tray lined with oiled baking parchment; the fruit should be about 0.5cm (¼ inch) thick. Cook for 10 hours.

3. The fruit should look like leather and peel easily away from the baking parchment. It might need longer in the middle, you can check by seeing if the whole thing peels away.

4. Take out of the oven and allow to cool. Cut strips widthways and roll up. I like to hold the rolls in place with cocktail sticks – hence the snails – or pop them all on a kebab stick.

These keep in a sealed container for two weeks, if they last that long!
For recipe photograph see page 148.

Note:
I tend to make a whole ovenful to make the most of the oven being on for this length of time, or make oven-dried tomatoes (see page 163) at the same time.

SUGAR-FREE

8
Drying

Drying

Drying or dehydration is probably the easiest of all the preserving techniques and one that can be used for so many things. It has been used as a method for preserving for thousands of years and dried foods have had an important part to play in the nutrition of many civilisations.

Dehydrating works by inhibiting bacterial and other microbial growth by removing or reducing the water content of a food.

No special equipment is required at all, although you can go down that route if you get more deeply into it or want to make larger quantities. There are several ways to dry foods to allow them to be stored for use at a later date without specialist equipment:

— **An airing cupboard** can be used to dry most things
— **A sunny spot outside**, as long as it is safe to leave without it being bothered by curious wildlife
— **A warm radiator** will also work
— **Some ovens** these days have a drying/dehydrating setting on them, which is great, but if not the lowest setting will also work

Herbs are probably where most people will start. Even someone without a garden can have a window box or work surface with a pot of herbs growing. The excess herbs can be dried to use later in the season, or you can forage for plants that can be useful in the kitchen. Herbs for cooking or herbs and plants for teas are easy and quick to dry. Fruits can be dried to save them for later in the season. After all, that is what prunes and raisins are.

Points to consider when drying produce

— All the pieces should be a similar size so they dry at the same rate
— The rate at which they dry needs to be fast enough that the food doesn't deteriorate in quality before it is dry enough – air circulation is important in helping that process

Oven-dried tomatoes <small>JG</small>

There is a time of year when tomatoes take over, and it's great to have lots of different ways of preserving them for the cold winter months. If you live somewhere with a consistent hot, dry summer then you could sun-dry them, but in Wales the conditions require an oven! These dried tomatoes are delicious nibbled as they are, just like a sweet, and gorgeous in salads and on pizzas and pasta.

Makes 300ml (1¼ cups)

—

450g (1lb) cherry tomatoes, cut in half or quarters if large (try and make similar-sized pieces)
Salt and pepper to taste
Sprig of thyme, leaves picked off

1. Preheat oven to its lowest setting.

2. Place the tomatoes on a tray and sprinkle with the salt and pepper and thyme leaves.

3. Leave in the oven for 10 hours until fully dried out and wrinkled up. Check through them as some larger pieces may need to be left in longer. Cool and store in a jar in a cool, dark cupboard.

These will keep for up to six months.

Maple apple crisps MB

I originally saw these on Alana Chernila's wonderful blog 'Eating from the ground up'; she had in turn found them on the Simple Bites blog written by Aimée Wimbush-Bourque. They are so delicious they should not be missed and make a great healthy snack that doesn't hang around for long. They take a while to dry but barely any of it is active time.

Never makes quite enough as they are eaten so fast!
—

5–6 apples
60ml (4 tbsp) maple syrup
Juice of half a lemon
½ tsp mixed spice

1. Preheat the oven to 110°C / 225°F / Gas mark ¼.

2. Core the apples and slice into very thin slices. A mandolin does this best but a very sharp knife will do.

3. Mix the maple syrup, lemon juice and mixed spice in a medium bowl. Add the apple slices and mix well to coat them with the liquid. Remove and allow them to drain a little in a colander so any excess liquid drips off.

4. Line 2 baking trays with parchment and place apples in a single layer (see photograph on page 158).

5. Place in the oven for 2–3 hours until dry and almost crisp. They will continue to crisp a little as they cool. The exact time will depend on how thin you managed to cut your apple slices, and also their water content and how much of the maple syrup mixture you drained off.

6. Take out of the oven to cool. Pack in an airtight container.

These will last for a couple of weeks … if you don't eat them faster. They are so delicious it will be hard to keep them longer anyway.

About the Authors

Anja Dunk grew up in the Welsh countryside where homegrown produce and wild foraging were part of daily life. Here began her love for preserving. She now lives with her young family just outside London where she is a caterer and freelance cook.

Mimi Beaven and her husband Richard founded the brand Made In Ghent a few years ago. For them, preserving the flavours of the year's harvest is essential preparation for the cold winter months on the family farm they are rebuilding in the Hudson Valley, New York. They raise pigs, bees and chickens. Mimi bakes sourdough and cooks seasonal goods in the farm kitchen, which are then sold to the local community from their farm store.

Jen Goss lives on a smallholding in West Wales with her family, following a lifelong dream to live by the sea and work the land. The produce of Jen's land and surrounding hedgerows provides ample supplies for Our Two Acres – the catering company she set up after a career in the hospitality industry in London.

Thanks

Firstly our thanks goes to **Clare Hieatt**, who brought us all together when our publisher Miranda West was looking for suitable authors; a true inspiration and fabulous lady, we wouldn't be here without her!

Richard Beaven, for his patience – especially during a lovely two-day photoshoot in West Wales – and for being a great teacher and wonderful photographer.

Miranda, for being our anchor throughout this process. Thanks for everything.

Jen

Colin Mathew, my partner in life, for trying everything I put in front of him, and somehow managing to always pass comment when I'm not always that great at receiving criticism.

Leon and **Lucy** – our kids have always inspired me to create new and delicious things for them to enjoy.

Teresa and **Julian Goss** – the knowledge I have and desire to cook everything and try anything comes straight from my mother and father. Growing up eating in the Goss household was a culinary education – and it still is.

Elizabeth Montefiore, my maternal grandmother – a kitchen full of wonder and joy, she was always experimenting and cooking for many, and has inspired me throughout my life.

All my local friends in West Wales who have provided produce to experiment with.

Mimi

Richard – my husband, business partner and the 'voice of reason' in my life. Thank you for encouraging me to do things I never thought I could, for not complaining as much as you might have, and for taking the most wonderful photos for this book.

Meg and **Martha** – our daughters, who have been patient(ish) throughout a period of 'inconsistent meals' while I was busy cooking for what seemed like everybody but them.

Jacques and **Jenny Astic** (my parents) and **Marcel** and **Marie-Therese Astic** (my paternal grandparents) for giving me my love of cooking food and feeding people and an incredible work ethic.

All the amazing farmers who live and work so hard in our community growing the wonderful produce I get to cook with (and eat) every week.

Anja

Steven – my husband, thank you for always encouraging, questioning and pushing me.

Lucas, **Bia** and **Aidan** – my boys and favourite recipe testers, thank you for being interested in the recipes in this book.

Eveline and **Patrick** – my parents, thank you for being brilliant and helping me follow my passions in life. Mum, you are my one true inspiration.

Ursula, my Omi, and **Hedel**, my great-grandmother, who lived in a time where preserving was part of everyday life – thank you for your recipes.

My sister-in-law **Vera** and dear friends **Phoebe** and **Jen** – I am constantly inspired by your ways of cooking and incredible food, thank you.

Opposite
Jen in her poly-tunnel
Below
Mimi and Anja with rhubarb
donated by a kind neighbour

Index

INDEX